RESET

How to get paid
and love what you do

Dustin Peterson

Cover Design by Bryan Peterson at Peterson Ray & Company
311 N. Market Street | Suite 311
Dallas, TX 75202
www.peterson.com

ISBN-13: 978-1502392114
ISBN-10: 1502392119

DEDICATION

For Samye, who put up with the Great Reset of 2005 and
biennial resets every few years thereafter—

And for anyone who believes it's possible to do what you
love and get paid to do it. Guess what? You're right.

CONTENTS

ACKNOWLEDGMENTS

I'm indebted to a tribe of committed people who opened their hearts and minds to make this book happen.

In 2004, at a Whataburger on Greenville Avenue in Dallas, Texas, Clark Elliston blew my mind when he made it clear that he had no intention of pursuing a conventional, society-approved career path. At the time, I was doing just that. That conversation opened my eyes.

Matt Broadbent sent my career on a whole new trajectory in 2005 when I left public relations to figure out my life. Without his support, friendship, and inspiration, this book would never have begun.

Lindsey Thaler launched this book into existence in 2008 by inspiring me to write down my thoughts on career. Until I met Lindsey, I had never considered myself a writer but she gave me the confidence to believe that what I had to offer was worth sharing with the world. She re-launched it into existence with some timely and extensive feedback in 2010 and 2014.

Matt Evans was a consistent accountability partner that never doubted that I could complete this project. It's amazing what a few words of belief from a talented writer can do to build your confidence.

Trent Navran reignited my passion for the message in 2011 through countless conversations about the value of pursuing what you do best, while many others made it into the book as anecdotes and characters.

Aaron Smith swooped in two years ago and led me to the finish line. His support helped strip away my perfectionism and move the book along.

Others may not be in the book but supported me from the sidelines, including my mom, my in-laws, and other family members. My daughter, Halle, is one of my biggest fans! Thank you for your belief.

My deepest gratitude goes to my sweet wife, Samye, who told me along the way to just "write the blasted book already!" You were and are my rock. You lived this book. Every second of it. You've been in the trenches and have ridden this roller-coaster as only a best friend and eternal companion could – with grace, love, and unyielding belief.

And, of course, thank you to the greatest catalyst for my decade of career shifting: my dad. In 10th grade, I wrote a profile for the school newspaper on my dad and his business, music, and other entrepreneurial pursuits. We sat side-by-side on a plane trip and I interviewed him about his life for more than two hours. I came away impressed and inspired by his commitment to doing what he loves and adding value to the world. That conversation stuck with me. In 2004, he lit the same fire in me that burned in him – a drive to do what I do best and love what I do for a living. This fire has moved me ever since toward a rewarding career-path. My life will never be the same because of it.

INTRO

Imagine waking up each morning to get paid to be you. People simply want you to do what you do naturally well and they pay you good money to do it. That's a low-stress, high-reward way to live and it's not wishful thinking. I'm proof that it's possible.

But it's hard (and sometimes scary) to figure out on your own. What you need is someone who has been up the mountain and back. You need someone who has navigated more than a few paths and who can point out the pitfalls, the shortcuts, and the fastest route to the summit.

That's me. I'm your guide. I've been down the path and up it. And off it and back on again. I've reset my career many times – more than 12 to be exact – and I've learned a lot in the process. Now I'm passing on the knowledge.

In 2005, I quit my steady, corporate job to find a new, more meaningful life path. I knew there had to be a way to figure out what to do with my life and I was determined to

3

find it. I also decided that when I figured it out I would share it; I'd pass it down the path to others trying to make their way.

One year later, in 2006, I took the first major step to figuring it out by starting graduate school and launching my vocation, and I've been cruising down the path ever since, becoming more specialized in my work and loving what I do. The pathway that I took is in this book, as are stories and anecdotes from my own and others' experiences doing the same thing. I want to help you find something you love to do and do it!

If you're reading this book, you likely have one or more of the following questions:

1. How do I do what I love for a living?
2. What do I love to do?
3. How do I figure out what I love to do?
4. How can I love more of what I'm already doing?
5. Even if I do figure out what I love to do, can I make the leap to actually doing it and getting paid to do it?

I'll help you answer all five and probably even a few more you didn't even know you had. And here's the craziest part: whether you know it or not, **you already have all the tools you need to figure out what you love to do**. The answer isn't "out there" somewhere. You can figure it out now. The method is deceptively simple but the implementation is hard. This book will help you create a roadmap to get from where you are now to where you really want to be.

"Loving what you do for a living" is the key and it begs the question, "How do I figure it out and then do it?" This book answers that question.

This Ain't That

This book is not a manifesto about the type of life we could all be living if we just quit our jobs and followed our hearts with reckless abandon. Resets don't work like that. Figuring out your career path isn't an event, it's a journey. I started my career 10 years ago in public relations and now I teach, train, and coach leaders in all kinds of organizations. I didn't dive from PR into my current gig in leadership development in a week. It's taken years of time, energy, and investment to land in a truly satisfying career. There's give and take.

My first job was about 10% what I love to do and 90% what I loathe. By job #3 I was at 80% love and 20% loathe, and now I'm sitting right at 95% love. So if you bought this book expecting me to tell you to jump ship and become a blogger who makes money off Google Ads and travels the Andes, this book isn't for you.

Lots of authors have gone from rags to riches and they'll tell you how to do it too. They'll lay out the plan for going from living paycheck to paycheck to making a million. I've got bad news. That's not me.

What I've done is go from a totally unrewarding, decent paying job to a really fulfilling, great paying career – even a *vocation* or calling. I've worked with everyone from college students to millionaires. I've seen both sides and I can tell you that money only makes you happy to a point.

More on that later.

What I've figured out – my success story – is how to harness an immense amount of energy, motivation, and happiness doing something I love and making more than enough to support my family, save for the future, and live an abundant life. If that's what you want – abundance while living authentically – this is your book.

Think about it: if you could make what you make now or even more but drastically increase your energy and satisfaction in your career, what would that do for your life, your family, your health, and your future? I'll show you how to get there.

This book also doesn't pretend to give you the answer. It's not a quick-fix solution. When I career-coached students at Rice University I would occasionally have a student wander in saying, "I heard you can help me know what to do for a career. So what should I do?" If only it was that easy.

Figuring out your life path takes work – really hard work. It's not the type of work you may be used to but it's work nonetheless. If it was easy everyone would do it. I can't tell you what to do with your life, but I can tell you how to figure it out. I'll teach you how to fish, but you have to hook the bait, cast the lines, show some patience, and reel in the big one when the time comes.

This is This

There are several great books out there about career and how to figure out what to do with your life. A few I would recommend are *The $100 Startup*, *The War of Art*,

EntreLeadership, and *What Should I Do With My Life?* One general theme of most of these books is the same – if you do what you love, you will find satisfaction. My book echoes those sentiments.

However, most of these books also fall short in the same area. They don't offer practical, actionable guidance about *how* to figure out what to do with you life. What *is* your passion?

If you had asked me this question 12 years ago I would have said bacon, basketball, and dating. I'm trying to imagine a career path that might include all three but nothing comes to mind (at least nothing within my grasp). This book is built on the idea of helping you first figure out your passion and then find the confidence and know-how to go and do it.

This book is a jumpstart and a roadmap. This is a **mindset** book. I'm all about shifting your self-perception and helping you understand the principles of figuring out your life path. I believe that if you learn and apply the lessons in this book you will not only find your custom-fit career, one that pertains directly to your talent set, but that you will also do it more quickly than I did and with better results.

Imagine it: you invest less than one year of your life to find your true passion and become trained in it only to spend the rest of your career basking in it, reaping satisfaction, succeeding financially, and experiencing the joy that comes with doing something that aligns with who you are as an individual. The best part is it's never too late to start.

In reality, depending on the career path and the person, I believe the transition can happen much, much sooner and at any point in your life. Sometimes the best-fit career is right under your nose but there is this big ugly thing called fear standing in the way. A push over the edge is all you need and almost overnight you can be more fulfilled. If you're in it for the long-haul or you just need the push, this book will set you up for success.

I'm here to push you over the cliff.

Who This Book is For

Whether you're just starting out, perhaps as a freshman or sophomore in college, or you are a mid-career professional considering a career change, this book will show the steps to follow to get where you want to go.

That said, this book won't be for everyone. I believe it has value for every person, but I've also come to accept that not all people are seeking the same thing. Many individuals are content having a job for the sake of having a job. They work to live, so to speak, toiling away from 9-5 so that they can take their earnings and enjoy life outside of work. It's taken some time but I've come to understand this mentality.

This book is for the other half – those who feel a drive to not only be successful in their careers, but to also enjoy them and find satisfaction in their work. I can't imagine spending 40 hours a week doing something I hate...40 hours! I used to think that this was simply a reality for some people – for me! Now I know it is within our power to take control of our situation and harvest more energy in our daily lives.

Reflection

Throughout this book, I've included questions for you to reflect on and answer. As you work through these questions, I would recommend writing the answers down on paper, in a journal, or in an online notebook of some sort. There is something powerful about writing things down that helps to cement them in your mind.

After a few days of doing this, you will find that your self-awareness will increase and you will also see opportunities around you to enhance your energy and effectiveness by replicating the things that make you happy. More importantly, you will begin to see themes emerge that you can use as a guide or filter to screen potential careers or life choices – to figure out what to do with your life. Replicating the things that give you energy will lead to greater joy and happiness.

One of the keys to being able to make the leap to your dream career is to develop a network of support. Perhaps you already have a support network around you. If so, that's fantastic. Share your experiences with them as you work through this book. Others may be unsure of who your support system includes. Either way, I invite you to participate in the online community I've developed for this book. You can go to www.dustinpeterson.me and find like-minded people doing the same thing – pursuing passion. You can keep track of your answers to the questions in the book and begin to build your roadmap with a community of other readers who are also trying to make the change.

Enough preamble. Let's dive in.

Dustin Peterson

"Rising, streetcar, four hours in the office or the factory, meal, streetcar, four hours of work, meal, sleep, and Monday Tuesday Wednesday Thursday Friday and Saturday according to the same rhythm–this path is easily followed most of the time. But one day the 'why' arises and everything begins in that weariness tinged with amazement."

-Albert Camus,
The Myth of Sisyphus

Dustin Peterson

1. CATALYST

In 2004, I was a novice Account Coordinator at one of
the largest public relations agencies in the nation. What does
that mean? It means I edited documents, wrote press
releases using a template, and did a heap of cold calling on
behalf of my clients, one of which was GlaxoSmithKline,
the maker of Beano – "For Bloating and Gas!"

Let me repeat that...a ton of cold calling...about flatulence.

I actually represented five clients on the Healthcare and
Hospitality team, but Beano was my...favorite. My job was
to call media in the health and wellness industry and
journalists with newspapers and trade journals and convince
them to report the important new discovery that Beano
doesn't just fight gas, it can be used to treat Complex
Carbohydrate Intolerance, or gas from carb overload.
Translation: Eat too much broccoli and you'll be gassy.
Beano can save the day.

Tough sell.

Journalists hate receiving these calls. I hated making them. I had a window of about 10 seconds to make my point before they'd hang up on me. What's worse, the room where I made these calls was an oversized Tomb of Rejection. It looked like a panic room with a window.

It also didn't help that I was preconditioned with a low tolerance for rejection. One of my first jobs in high school was to cold call people. I showed up on the first day not knowing what I'd be doing. When I found out it was cold calling, I felt sick. I called a woman in Arkansas and interrupted her dinner to ask her to take a survey. She was livid, lit me up, and hung up. I made two more calls, excused myself to the restroom, and walked right out the back door and straight to my car. I never went back for my paycheck, which would have been about 65 cents for the seven minutes of work I did.

And yet, here I was again, eight years later and still cold-calling but with a bachelor's degree on my dossier. I laugh in hindsight to think about how seriously I took the whole thing. In fact, I can't believe how seriously everyone took it. We were crusading against gas. And no one, myself included, ever broke character. To us, it was the launching of a space shuttle into orbit or curing an incurable disease. It's amazing to think about now.

The call that finally broke me – the last straw – happened around mid-November. That afternoon, I'd been cold-calling for hours and I was more than 40 contacts in. My nerves were shot, my throat was dry, and I was reaching a breaking point. I felt like this next call would either be "the one" or it would send me into a tailspin ending in me blacking out from rejection and being left in the Tomb for days before anyone discovered me. It was short and simple and went like this:

"Hi there, this is Dustin calling on behalf of Beano. Is this a bad time?"

Pause. "Uh, yes. What do you need?" the voice said.

"Well, it turns out there's this thing called CCI that affects millions of Americ…"

"You're talking about farts, right?" he interjected.

"Well…kind of," I explained. "It's called Complex Carbohydrate Intolerance, Dave, and Beano is one of the few products on the market that can…"

"Haha. Yeah. No, thanks." Click.

Rejection. Again. These guys didn't want gas remedies. They wanted to be left alone. And I was sick of being the one trying to convince them otherwise. Let the world be gassy. I couldn't take it anymore. This last call broke me. Simple as it was, I couldn't do it. The phone seemed to weigh a thousand pounds.

What I didn't realize at the time was that this moment, this phone call, would become pivotal – a turning point. You've likely experienced one of these too. I call them catalytic moments, and paying attention to them is mission critical if you're going to do what you love for a living.

Recognizing Catalytic Moments

I recently heard a story on National Public Radio called "Why A Brush With Death Triggers The Slow-Mo Effect" about these pivotal moments. When individuals are faced with life or death situations, for a brief moment time seems to slow down. A fall from a building that seems like 10 seconds really only takes three. After the incident, the individual in the situation can describe every detail down to the smell of the air, the colors of sky, and the passersby.

Research shows that the memory kicks into high gear in these adrenaline-filled, near-death moments. While generally an efficient function that screens out unnecessary detail, the human mind instantaneously expands to take in every detail of the moment.

According to David Eagleman, a researcher who studies these moments, it's all about memory. "Normally, our memories are like sieves," he says. "We're not writing down most of what's passing through our system." But in this moment, "memory shifts gears. Now it's writing down everything — every cloud, every piece of dirt, every little fleeting thought, anything that might be useful."

Pitching media stories about gas must be the closest thing to death I've experienced because I was overwhelmed by heightened sensory perception: the dull ringing of the phone, the outdated and poorly imitated Renaissance painting on the cover of the phone book, the neon highlighter on my battered call list, and most importantly, the distinct, almost audible voice in my head lamenting – no, yelling – "What in the world are you doing with your life!?!" I can picture it in my mind's eye distinctly and it makes me shudder.

The Beano call was *the* moment that I made up my mind. Something had to give.

Each of us experiences these moments of clarity, when time stops, the busyness doesn't seem to matter, a light shines down in our minds, and we ask ourselves, Why? Why am I doing what I'm doing? What am I getting from this experience? Is this what I want to do? These are **catalytic moments**. If we pay attention to them, they have great power to motivate significant change in our lives.

Catalyze is a powerful word. It means to cause, inspire, or bring about significant change. These moments – catalytic – can ignite us on a whole new path if we'll listen. But *only* if we listen.

Resets are built on catalytic moments. Resets are do-overs. They're opportunities to stop the madness, re-direct the train, and head off in a new direction. The challenge is that we usually won't or don't or can't heed these catalytic moments because the voice of the world is too loud.

In these moments, our inner self is screaming to our outer self that something isn't right. It's in these moments that our true self seems to confront our inauthentic self and we have the potential to emerge from the inner conflict with resolution to live more congruently with our values. Sometimes we win the conflict, other times we don't.

You may be experiencing a catalytic moment right now. That may have been what prompted you to read this book.

You know it when you feel it – it's that moment when you stop running the race and ask yourself if you're on the right track. You put on the brakes, pull to the shoulder, and look around at the crazies blowing by you and wonder how you ever got on the track in the first place. If you've experienced a catalytic moment, pay attention. It may be time to move in a different direction.

Step one to figuring out what you love to do and doing more of it is to pay attention to that Inner Voice that says, "Wake up. This isn't you. There's got to be more." What's even more powerful is that the Inner Voice often tells you what you should be doing instead. In fact, it's probably told you over and over but you've blocked it for one reason or another. We'll talk about that later.

But for now, can you identify catalytic moments in your life? Odds are you can think of one or two right away. Write them down – the moments that have told you that it might be time for something else. Start keeping track of the moments when your Inner Voice is telling you that it is time to make change. In fact, start now by jotting down a few notes on the next page. Don't move on until you do. Acceptance of reality is always step one.

Chapter 1 Reflection

Can you think of catalytic moments you've had in your life? What were they? Jot them down here.

What was your Inner Voice telling you in these moments?

What is your Inner Voice telling you now?

Deep down, have you always had an inkling about what you were meant to do with your life? Have you done it at all? Why or why not?

"The things you are passionate about are not
random, they are your calling."
–Fabienne Fredrickson

2. THE BREAKING POINT

If you're like me, you've had many catalytic moments screaming "wake up!" You've also ignored them. Recognizing them is step one, but it's only step one. I ignored them repeatedly. In fact, it took a meltdown to shake me out of it.

My wife was cooking at the stove of our beat down apartment near downtown Dallas in 2004. As newlyweds we lived in a poorly lit complex in the obligatory dumpy "first apartment." I had been valiantly working my new job in public relations for several months, slaying dragons for my new bride who was passing time eradicating fleas as a veterinary assistant at a local clinic. We had recently found out she was pregnant and we were overjoyed by the prospect of welcoming a little addition to our family.

One day, shortly after my catalytic moment in the Tomb of Rejection, I walked into the "dining room" – which was really an extension of the living room but with a table in the middle of it – to chat with my wife. She was stirring something in the steel pot that I'm sure smelled fantastic. I couldn't relish it because all of my senses were keyed in on the pent up negative energy that was boiling just below my surface.

I leaned against the wall, partly to appear unassuming but mostly to support the invisible weight of the nearly-palpable negativity that was bearing down on my shoulders.

We had completed all of the steps society prescribes. After graduating from college, we moved back to Texas to be close to family; I was working a stable, corporate job in the field that I majored in; and we were preparing to welcome a baby into our young family.

At the same time, each of these steps represented deeper roots in a ground that had become suddenly shaky. Like the downward torque of a screw in wood, each decision we were making seemed to be increasing the inner tension that I felt and shortening the time that I had to make a significant course correction. If you've ever worked a job you disliked for a significant period of time, you know the feeling. I started to feel suffocated, like every day was further cementing my future and I was decreasing the likelihood that I could ever jump ship. If I ignored the obvious any longer, the wood might split.

"How was your day?" she asked, innocently enough.

I couldn't release the tension yet. I couldn't overwhelm her so suddenly. I have yet to understand the intricacies of pregnancy, but a pregnant woman with a firm grip on a boiling pot of hot liquid plus a dash of "I hate my job" sounds like a potentially dangerous situation.

I let the invisible weight press down on my body as I slid down the wall and into a crumpled ball on the floor. My wife looked up at the sight of her lanky, 6'5" husband in a tight ball on the ground and, with a quizzical look and an obvious shift in her tone, asked, "What's wrong?"

I couldn't contain the simmering of emotion and the feelings boiled over. I started to cry. One of those whimpering sobs that makes you feel weak and vulnerable. My vision was blurred and I couldn't make out the expression on my wife's face, but I'm certain it was a mix of shock, disorientation, surprise (that my tear ducts still functioned), and concern. I was broken.

To put this in context, I only cried three times in the first six years of my marriage – six years! Of course, I've cried more than a dozen times in the last four years, mostly because of well-placed body blows from my kids while wrestling. But this time was a gusher that counts for future tears for at least a decade.

On the one hand, it felt like a good release. On the other, it was totally humbling and a bit humiliating at the same time. I was to be the main source of income going forward in our family – the breadwinner. And yet, here I was, 45 degrees away from being completely in the fetal position.

Between sniffles and utter meltdown I muttered the secret that had stewed in me since we had moved back to Texas. I had bottled it up because I didn't want to disrupt society.

"I hate my job."

I had rarely felt so vulnerable yet so authentic. As humbling as it was to admit my weakness, it was energizing to call it like it was. I should have started this story with an ode to my wife. Let me take a second here to hit home an important point: no career move, especially major transition, will happen without the support of at least one ally – a spouse or some other advocate. You simply can't go it alone. It's too long of a journey, and often a dark and risky one at that. Find a friend, a supporter, a colleague, or someone to talk to as you work through the process. Find a tribe of like-minded people who can encourage you when the road gets tough. The reason I wrote this book is to let you know that you have at least one ally in the world who doesn't think you're crazy – me.

My wife is my best friend and ultimate ally, and she nailed the response. "Ok, then, let's quit and try something else." Calm, cool, collected. Wow. Where we are today is due to her support, love, empathy, and patience. She's put up with a lot and it's paid off. Find someone who believes in you and enroll them in your goal. It'll pay huge dividends.

You don't need to be at the point of crumbling to the floor in a ball but you do need to feel enough burn to desire to change your current situation. Figuring out your life path is actual work. There are steps you have to take, energy you have to devote, and risks that take you outside of your comfort zone. Sometimes risk is dramatic.

We suddenly had a huge decision to make and two options we were considering:

A. Continue toiling away in PR and see where it took me.
B. Quit my job, move into the unknown, hopefully find a job, and hopefully succeed in order to provide for my wife and newborn child. And, if not, then hopefully I could figure out a new life-path. Note the overuse of the word "hopefully." It was intentional.

Option A was the obvious choice, and comfortable. But option B was the *only* choice. I couldn't live incongruently any longer.

In hindsight, I was working in an industry with a serious values rub. Not that the industry itself was misguided, but the alignment with my values system was out of whack. I needed to work with people, to empower them, to teach and facilitate and coach and train. I needed an extraverted, ever-changing environment. Instead I was in the exact opposite situation.

We pulled the trigger and began to plan for option B and it was scary and anxiety-ridden and unknown. But it was the best decision we ever made career-wise. I shudder to think where I would be now, more than 10 years later, had I chosen option A.

Dave Ramsey says, "Where you are now is an accumulation of decisions you have made up to this point. If you don't like where you are, make different decisions starting today!"

So you've really got two choices right now: double-down on what you are currently doing or hit the reset button and try something new, something closer to who you are. One thing I've learned in my career is that the "reset" button will not be ignored. I've also learned that you are never too young or old to hit the button. Whether you are a sophomore in college resetting a major or a mid-career professional resetting your career path, it's always possible. Whether you hit it now or in your 60's, your inner self demands to be acknowledged and you'll eventually pursue your strengths in your work.

Hearing the Inner Voice

We decided to hit reset. After months of being dutiful in a job I disliked we finally made the wisest choice we could have: we listened to the Inner Voice. In fact, I've learned throughout the course of my journey that listening to the Inner Voice is key. Let me illustrate how it works. I've tuned mine out many times over the years. I've also listened to it from time to time and had great results from it.

To illustrate, let me take you back to the time when I almost pursued my passion and saved myself 10 years of searching – but didn't.

The First Time I Knew

It was a Sunday in 2001. I was 21. I had been home from my LDS mission for five months. My first responsibility in our student congregation was as a Sunday School teacher and I loved it almost instantly. I got a rush from preparing a really great lesson with humor and in a way that kept peoples' interest. I loved presenting to the group and conveying Gospel topics in a way that was easy to understand and relate to. I'd be lying if I didn't admit that I thrived on the attention. I also thrived on the competition of being the best class. My peers had several class options but mine became the go-to choice. Some days I would have 100 people in the class.

On this particular Sunday it must have been parent's weekend because I had a glut of mothers in the group. I prepared a great lesson on Joseph and the coat of many colors. I wore a rainbow-striped robe and the lesson flowed really well. Afterward, two moms came up to me. One said that I should really consider a job teaching seminary for the LDS Church. The moment she said it I felt this rush of energy. It was the first time I had considered that I could get paid to do this every day. What a concept. Note, by the way, that catalytic moments are both positive and negative and positive ones are almost always accompanied by a rush of energy. You feel them.

Little did I know then that I would one day spend almost every day in front of groups of people, teaching lessons with humor and in a way that kept peoples' interest. I would engage people in learning for a living. This Sunday moment is significant, because I knew in my core that I wanted to do this, and yet it took almost 10 years to come back around to it.

My Inner Voice was telling me "this is right." I walked out of each class feeling alive. In fact, all week I would think about what I was going to teach on Sunday. I knew this is what I was meant to be doing.

This seems like a no-brainer. I know. Surely I enrolled in a teaching class and the rest is history, right? Actually, the wheels came off in devastating fashion a mere two months later. Again, you might be able to relate.

I registered for the seminary pre-service class to learn to teach seminary for a living. I vividly remember showing up on the first day and seeing a room full of 40 dynamic, energized, and well-equipped teachers. The pre-service trainer shared with us that only five of us would ever make it through the whole process and as I sat at the back of the room looking around I felt totally discouraged. I had no confidence that I would be one of them. Several of these classmates seemed to already have inroads with the trainer and each other. I felt hopeless. I persisted through the class and met all of the requirements but bailed after one semester on the remainder of the program. I simply lacked the confidence.

This is when I decided to get serious about a "real" major. This was the moment when I sold out on the Inner Voice for the first time. I would play along with what I knew was the responsible thing to do and get a real job.

The Voice of Resistance

Sometimes we talk ourselves out of doing the very things we are best at doing. A cruel paradox exists in the world of talent which is that those things that we are most talented at are often the things we feel least confident doing. I'm not sure why this is, but you hear stories of athletes, musicians, politicians, and others who are immersed in utter fear right before they do what they do best. It fuels them in the end, but if we aren't ready for it, this fear can derail us from doing what we do best. We end up just exploring it on the side as a hobby or not at all.

I looked around the room of 40 prospects and said, "No way I'M gonna be one of the five. What's the point." Truth is, who knows? For all I know I could have been top three or number one, but I gave in to another voice.

The reality is that there are two internal voices working to influence your decisions. The Inner Voice is the one you should always follow. The second voice is what Steven Pressfield, author of one of my all-time favorite reads, *The War of Art*, calls the Resistant Voice, which always comes right on the heels of the Inner Voice. Always. You know both of them I'm sure. Here's an example of one of the frequent conversations my Inner Voice and Resistant Voice have:

> **Inner Voice:** "You should start a company and career coach people into using their strengths more in their careers. You have a gift for this."

> **Resistant Voice:** "Right. That's not going to work. Who would be your clients? Could you actually make enough to survive? And how would you even do it? Your family will starve. And then you will have left a good job. And you'll end up in a worse job with worse pay and worse benefits doing something you hate. Better to stay put."

You've got to understand – and this is key – that on the heels of every "eureka!" moment from your Inner Voice comes the Voice of Resistance that immediately tells you why you can't. It never fails. Try it. Think of what you would do if you could do anything. Let your mind go and imagine it. Now pause.

Hear that? Those thoughts that begin to creep in and tell you why that isn't realistic? Resistance. In fact, when I coach people on pursuing their passion I actually listen for the "but" that's getting in the way of them doing what they really want to do. That's what they pay me to explore. I've learned over time that what lies on the other side of the "but" is sometimes realistic and a rational reason to not pursue what they want to pursue, but the line between realism and pursuing your passion is thin and dangerous to walk. Err on the side of pursuing passion.

Society and the Resistant Voice

Oddly, it seems as though the Resistant Voice is also deeply in tune with what society thinks. This was another factor in my decision to ditch my dream to teach seminary and stick with the "safe route."

As I was getting into teaching seminary I talked with a close mentor about my plans. Colin was a doctor-in-training. His dad had been a physician, his older two siblings were physicians and he was on the fast-track through medical school to follow in the family tradition. Despite only being a half-decade older than me, he seemed to have it all figured out. Reality was that he hated biology, had no interest in medicine, and had real passion for music and was a talented cellist. But he would never have shared this with anyone.

Colin was a respected mentor of mine. My confidant. I not only shared my ideas with him but I relied on his guidance. I figured Colin could relate with my desire to teach seminary.

It started with him innocently asking me what my plan was when I graduated. It felt good to talk about it. I felt whole, congruent. I couldn't wait to share it. But an interesting thing happened when I told him about my dream. He furrowed his brow and said flatly, "You can't support a family doing that. What else are you considering?"

That rocked me. I respected Colin's opinion a lot. I quickly jumped to my back up plan – public relations – which he was only slightly more impressed with. After this conversation I felt empty. Maybe Colin was right. Seminary was a dead-end job for raising a family. I decided to ditch seminary once and for all and just focus on the PR path.

A few simple words of discouragement added more weight to the list of reasons my Resistant Voice had already come up with for not pursuing my dream: the road would be hard, you can't support a family, you're not really that good anyway.

The only thing worse than talking yourself out of pursuing a pathway is letting someone else do it. Especially someone with no actual knowledge or expertise in your area or in who you are.

Everyone has an opinion. In fact, I've learned that there are at least three types of people who chime in on dreams:

1) Those who support you – they are often quiet but loyal.

2) Those who are indifferent – they are quiet, disinterested, and passive supporters.

3) The naysayers – they are the most vocal and seem to

consider it their job to bring you back down to reality. They are dangerous precisely because they are the most vocal.

One of the most challenging things about pursuing your passion for a career is the number of naysayers that emerge and say things like, "it doesn't matter what you do, as long as you do it well." Bull. For me, the combo of self-doubt and self-talk and the opinion of a third party was all it would take to break me. PR it would be. The Inner Voice lost that battle.

I bailed on the seminary aspirations. As soon as I graduated in August of 2004, my new wife and I moved to Dallas so that I could find a job in PR and we could be closer to family. After settling in, I pounded the pavement, sending out resumes and cover letters, attending conferences, and working my network. It was horrible.

I had a good background in PR from my undergrad program but in hindsight I didn't care about the field. I was trying to land a job in something that I couldn't care less about and it felt empty. Sure enough, I landed a position through a contact at church at The Firm and started in September 2004. I disliked it almost immediately. And I never really learned to like it. In fact, each day I felt less and less authentic, more tired and bored, and less driven. My wife must have wondered who she had married.

Gone were the days of fun and dynamic Dustin and frequent were the days of soulless Dustin. In fact, I would shower the night before work each day and then lay out my work clothes next to the bed. I had to be at work by 8:30am so I would set my alarm for 7:58am to get up, throw on my clothes, grab cereal on my way out, and get to work. I was totally unmotivated to get up and get going because I disliked it.

This brings me to the infamous flatulence call. The moment that catalyzed my career change. I knew that Account Coordinator wasn't the job for me. The trick is, I also knew there could be something more. I grew up in a home with a dad who was an entrepreneur. He loved his job and got paid really well to do it. I knew because of my dad's example that it was possible for me to get paid to do something I loved to do. Some people supported the idea, but most thought I should just bite the bullet and get a real job. Naysayers.

The Moment

So I hit up my old man for some advice on our way to a Dallas Cowboys game in 2005. What he said during that car ride changed my life.

We had been going to sports games for years as a form of bonding. On this night, we sat in tight traffic only a few miles from the stadium catching up on life. Unbeknownst to my dad, the invisible weight was bearing down on me. On the surface, things were progressing smoothly: Job? Check. Marriage? Definite check. Kids? Almost check – one on the way. Happy...?

Our conversation drifted to the topic of career. I had always respected my dad for his love of his job. In the 80's, when graphic design was a misunderstood and largely undeveloped industry, he had set out to establish a firm that would provide creative services for corporations and educational institutions. More importantly, he had been hugely successful in doing it and loved what he did for a living. He was unique because, like so few, he had discovered his life path and followed it. His life seemed so planned out. Mine was so disoriented.

After a few minutes of conversation, my dad asked, "How's your job?" I paused. I pretended to reflect for a moment as if to find the right words to describe it. The truth was that I already knew where I stood with my job. I had this same conversation with myself night after night for the past few months. I couldn't hide it.

"I don't like it," I said.

I would have said I hated it, but hate was a harsh word for a pre-game chat.

"It's not what I want to do. I'm doing well at it, and I receive praise from my supervisors, but I feel totally unsatisfied at the end of the day – totally exhausted." I thought about my routine for the past several months. Wake up. Go to work. Come home completely drained. Collapse onto my bed for at least half an hour. Try to muster the strength to get up and be a good husband. I felt like I might fall apart right there in the passenger seat.

He listened intently, likely searching for the right words to catch me in my tailspin and calm the storm that was brewing. He then asked me the golden question:

"Well, what would you want to do?"

I thought about it, again pretending that this was the first time I had considered another option. "I want to teach seminary. For the Church. I feel that this is my calling. When I think of teaching the Gospel for a living...wow."

He didn't hesitate. "Then why don't you do it?" he asked.

I had been convinced that I couldn't support a family on a seminary salary. By convinced, I mean that several people had suggested that I would never survive on a seminary teacher's salary and I allowed that to have impact on me. In reality, I probably would have been making more as a seminary teacher than I was with my PR firm. In hindsight, it's interesting how I took on the Resistant Voice as my own and actually defended it's rationale.

"I don't think I could make it work, financially," I stated. "I couldn't support a family. And what if it didn't work? Then where would I be?? Too many unknowns."

The silence dragged for a few seconds. Even before my dad started to speak, I could sense he was about to hit me with some serious old-guy wisdom.

He said, "Dustin, I learned from a respected friend, early in my career, an important piece of advice that has made all the difference. He once told me there are three types of people in most industries:

"Those at the bottom – These people aren't serious about a profession, think it will be easy, will make a moderate income, and will always struggle.

"Those in the middle – This level is jam-packed. These individuals either can't excel or don't want to because they are content with the status quo. They are generally solid workers who make a decent living but may never go higher.

"And those at the top – The upper levels are vacuous. There is plenty of room, big money, and less competition. These people are at the top for a very specific reason. Here is the reason, and I want you to remember this:

There is always room at the top for those who love what they do.

"If you love what you do, there will be a place for you the top of that industry regardless of the field. If you love to teach religion, then you will rise to the top as the best religion teacher the world has seen."

As he spoke, it felt like a curtain was lifted from my mind. "There is always room at the top for those who love what they do." Suddenly it was ok to do what I wanted. A world of new possibilities opened up and in this moment, this brief instant, my life changed. It seemed so simple and it was the validation that I needed from someone who had made it.

It gave me a charge – a mission – to do what I love. If I could just do that, the rest would sort itself out. That moment changed me.

I spent the next few years pursuing seminary and

continuing to figure out what I love to do, using my own career journey as a case study. The more I explored seminary I realized it wasn't the right fit. Not quite. But it led me to my just-right job. I've been all over the map working all kinds of jobs including the following:

- Wellness company
- Pest control sales
- Communications intern
- Alarm system technician
- Public relations practitioner
- Alarm system sales
- Customer service representative
- Large appliance delivery
- Community service intern
- Leadership coordinator

I've tried a few careers. However, I found my way to a best-fit career. I now teach and train leaders and managers to be more effective in their roles. I career coach individuals to help them find more satisfaction in their work. And I serve and teach in my church, fulfilling my desire to do what I love. I spend my days helping others maximize their potential and live more fulfilled lives!

The deeper I get and the more specialized I become, the more I love what I do every day and the more people want me to do it. I believe you can get paid to do what you love to do because I get paid to do what I love to do.

I also made a commitment that when I figured out how to get to the career I love, I would share my journey with the world to help others figure it out too. This book is that roadmap, the plan for how to get from where you are now to where you really want to be. It isn't theoretical or my hypothesis of what might work. It's what has worked for me and thousands of others and I believe it'll work for you too.

Let me preview the process for you:

1. People who love what they do are most happy and successful. Period.
2. Pay attention to the catalytic moments telling you to move on to something more congruent.
3. Figure out what you really love to do, and it's probably not what you think it is. You simply can't go wrong doing what you do best every day.
   a. Do the Inner Work which is all about identifying your talents to figure out what you do best.
   b. Do the Outer Work which is exposure to more people and things to find out where you can do what you do best and what it will take to get there.
   c. Watch out for fear and self-doubt, among other enemies of success. They especially creep up when you are on the edge of the dock getting ready to make the leap.
4. Figure out if you can do what you do best where you already are.
   a. If you can stay put and do more of what you love then figure out how to craft your

current experience to appeal to what you do best. By the way, most of us can modify our positions to appeal more to our strengths with some effort.

b. If not, figure out how much you need to make to be happy, your tolerance for risk, and how to make the transition smoother by beginning to do it now, then put yourself in a place to develop what you do best and make the leap to doing it in another place.

5. Do it! If you've bought into steps 1-4, this step is easier than it seems. Most of us try to do it without ever preparing for the leap.

This is the same process I use when career coaching people. They usually agree with number 1 before ever calling me and have felt the pull of number 2. Numbers 3 and 4 are where we spend our time. The fact is you can do what you love and get paid to do it and it is never too late for a reset. At the very least, you can move the needle on your current circumstances enough to catalyze more joy and happiness in your current career.

I'm here to help you do it. So let's do it.

Chapter 2 Reflection

As you were reading, I'll bet you were answering my dad's questions, weren't you? "Well, what do you want to do?" Let's start documenting now. Even if all you came up with was a single word to describe what you want to do, write it down. We'll continue to flesh it out as we go along in the book.

What do you want to do?

Why don't you do it?

"Your work is going to fill a large part of your life, and the only way to be truly satisfied is to do what you believe is great work. And the only way to do great work is to love what you do." –Steve Jobs

3. CASH MONEY

Catalytic moments can be incredibly difficult because they cause us to question the status quo, yet they can also be periods of immense creativity and clarity because we allow ourselves to let down our guard and begin to consider other options. We also dive into riskier ground – if only mentally – and consider careers and paths we may never otherwise consider. If we are to be happy and have joy, we must learn to capitalize on these moments and make change.

Pay attention to the environmental cues that are prompting you to move on in life! Most importantly, listen to the Inner Voice. Mine was telling me that I was becoming someone I didn't want to be. And yet I ignored it and pressed on out of a sense of duty. Wow. What a mistake.

The fact is, doing nothing will keep you on the path you're headed down. Doing something will alter the landscape just enough to send you down a different path. In order to find your way, you need a guide. Your Inner Voice is like your intuition. It has a sense of the direction you should follow.

There's one more voice I should bring up that is often more powerful than the Inner Voice and that had a big impact on our willingness to pursue my passion, and that's the voice of pending starvation.

Money and Resets

My hypothesis is that one of the big obstacles standing in the way of your reset is money. It has to be. You can't really survive without it. One of our biggest fears in making the leap was money. How would we survive? Here we were deciding to leave a stable profession for the unknown. Could we even afford to leave The Firm?

The lie that kept me paralyzed was this:

I'm not happy and it's killing me, but I feel like I have to do it to make money. There is no other way.

Here's the happy and surprising news: the amount of money you really need to make to be "happy" is very attainable. In fact, money can only buy happiness to a certain point.

One of the first things I often ask clients before I start career coaching is "how important is money to you?" This seems obvious but it's actually rather complex.

If values are the relative importance we give to the priorities in our lives, then you've got to figure out where on your priority list money falls. What comes before it and what comes after? If money is number one, then you know you'll need to pursue a career straightaway that will lead to high earnings. If, on the other hand, you can delay the comforts that money provides, then you free up many options that you otherwise may not have considered.

This concept of figuring out where money fits in your list of priorities reminds me of a story I heard several years ago. It took a little digging but here it is, attributed to "anonymous:"

"An American tourist was at the pier of a small coastal Mexican village when a small boat with just one fisherman docked.

"Inside the small boat were several large yellowfin tuna. The tourist complimented the fisherman on the quality of his fish and asked how long it took to catch them.

"The fisherman replied, 'Only a little while.'

"The tourist then asked, 'Why didn't you stay out longer and catch more fish?'

"The fisherman said, 'With this I have more than enough to support my family's needs.'

"The tourist then asked, 'But what do you do with the rest of your time?'

"The fisherman said, 'I sleep late, fish a little, play with my children, take siesta with my wife, Maria, stroll into the village each evening where I sip wine and play guitar with my amigos…I have a full and busy life.'

"The tourist scoffed, 'I can help you. You should spend more time fishing, and with the proceeds, buy a bigger boat. With the proceeds from the bigger boat you could buy several boats. Eventually you would have a fleet of fishing boats. Instead of selling your catch to a middleman you would sell directly to the processor; eventually opening your own cannery. You would control the product, processing and distribution. You could leave this small coastal fishing village and move to Mexico City, then Los Angeles and eventually New York where you could run your ever-expanding enterprise.'

"The fisherman asked, 'But, how long will this all take?'

"The tourist replied, '15 to 20 years.'

"'But what then?' asked the fisherman.

"The tourist laughed and said, 'That's the best part. When the time is right you would sell your company stock to the public and become very rich, you would make millions.'

"'Millions?…Then what?'

"The American said, 'Then you would retire. Move to a

small coastal fishing village where you would sleep late, fish a little, play with your kids, take siesta with your wife, stroll to the village in the evenings where you could sip wine and play your guitar with your amigos.'"

Money makes a poor leader, but a great follower. It's a great by-product, but not a great end-game. That said, money is important, and at some level we all value it. It's essential for survival. Thus, prior to sorting out your next career move you have to figure out where it fits for you. Is it a key driver? A backseat passenger? How much do you need to survive?

I was talking with a client about a year ago who is very talented, self-aware, and driven. He is bound to do great things in whatever field he chooses. I asked him what type of job he is looking for and he said, "Honestly, something that pays me money. That's it." It's tough to deny that this is a key factor for most people, after all, money makes the world go around. However, I would argue that this client will inevitably find a job that pays him money, and that when that basic need is fulfilled he will immediately begin to analyze that job according to how it fulfills his other needs. So how do you decide how important money is to you? Let me give an example and a concrete solution.

What's Your Threshold?

My wife and I were reviewing our finances several years ago, performing a financial check-up of sorts. We often felt like we were chasing a carrot on a string – as soon as we hit a new pay level our needs seemed to increase and we were left wanting more. This is sometimes referred to as the "hedonic treadmill," a phrase used to describe the habit of always looking at the person in the position higher than you, making more money than you, and wanting what they have. This is human nature. We usually couch this tendency in clichés such as "the grass is always greener on the other side of the fence."

The cruel irony of this habit or human tendency is that, as with a treadmill, you put a lot of energy into the pursuit without covering any ground – you may continue up the chain and make more money but never find lasting happiness or satisfaction. So it was with us.

We were trying to decide at what point we would be satisfied and able to push money to the side to focus on other sources of happiness. It occurred to me that we didn't know where we were headed. We were aiming at a moving target. So I suggested that instead of starting with what we make and aiming for what we wish we had, why not reverse the equation.

One way to figure out how important money is to you is to start by making a list of everything you would need on a monthly basis to feel satisfied. Don't leave anything out. Include all categories including mortgage, utilities, groceries, savings, vacation, clothing, etc. Then throw out a number, based on average past expenditures and informed by future desires, for each category. How much grocery money would be ideal? Clothing?

Lastly, add it all up. This is the big reveal – the amount you need to aim for to be truly satisfied. Our "ideal world" yearly budget, with all needs and wants accounted for, was

$77,631.60.

More importantly, though, what's yours? The number will be different for everyone. The goal is to establish your threshold now.

Once you've set the ideal amount – the top end of the range – set the bottom end of the range.

My buddy Matt asked me recently what the minimum is that I could live off of for a year if it came to that. How much could I afford while maintaining a good quality of life but cutting out non-essentials? This was eye-opening. I realized that if we really scaled back, meaning no money for savings or vacations or "extras" but simply to sustain life, we could get by for a year on around $55,000. Suddenly, with my range set – $55k to survive, $77k to thrive – I can more clearly make decisions about my career and my future.

The interesting thing about our top-of-range number is that it fits with the research on the link between money and happiness. It turns out that according to a study by some smart people at the University of New Jersey, money actually can affect happiness up to a certain point. In a survey of 1,000 Americans, researchers found that money equals satisfaction, but only to an extent. From the article:

"More money does not necessarily buy more happiness, but less money is associated with emotional pain," wrote Princeton University researchers Daniel Kahneman and Angus Deaton in the Proceedings of the National Academy of Sciences.

"Perhaps $75,000 a year is a threshold beyond which

47

further increases in income no longer improve individuals' ability to do what matters most to their emotional well-being, such as spending time with people they like, avoiding pain and disease, and enjoying leisure."

So $75,000 a year is the magic threshold where the amount of money you make can no longer really buy happiness, or said another way, where money can no longer ease the burdens that get in the way of well-being. Until you hit $75K, money can seem important because you need it to pay your bills and feed your family. But anything above the $75K mark really isn't necessary to do what you need it to do to be happy. At that point, well-being can be completely satisfied from a different place. At that point, it's up to you.

The Money/Happiness Continuum

I have a theory about money and happiness that is best illustrated by the diagrams below:

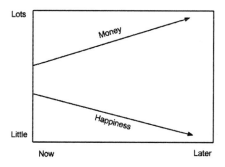

When you choose money over a job that makes you

happy, money and happiness operate on opposite trajectories. You may start out at a higher pay rate but over time as you make more money you become less happy. This isn't new. Stories abound of wealthy people who are unhappy because they've traded happiness and well-being for money.

In his book *True North*, Bill George confirmed the prevalence of this mentality:

"Many young leaders are tempted to take high-salaried jobs to pay off loans or build their savings, even if they have no interest in the work and do not intend to stay. They believe that after ten years they can move on to do the work they love. Yet many become so dependent on maintaining a certain lifestyle that they get trapped in jobs where they are demotivated and unhappy. Locked into the high-income/high-expense life, they cannot afford to do work they love. Ironically, not one of the leaders interviewed [for the book] wound up taking a position predicated upon establishing wealth early so that they could later pursue roles they would enjoy." (p. 111)

However, when you choose happiness over money, the two operate on the same trajectory – upward. The chart on the following page illustrates this concept.

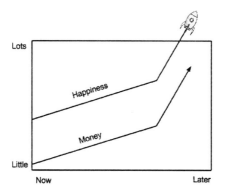

Note that you may start out making less money but your happiness is higher because you've chosen a job that makes you happy. You're not going to make less than you start out at, so no matter what, the trajectory is upward for your earning potential. In fact, as you grow in happiness, you become more successful and specialized in the thing that makes you happy.

Pay increases come steadily, albeit not large, and eventually you hit a tipping point. This occurs when the world discovers you for what you do – the thing that makes you happy and in which you've developed a specialization – and your happiness and money spike. You're now getting really well-compensated to do what you love. You make up less than 20% of the population at this point. Congratulations!

Bill George shared an example from Jean-Pierre Rosso, former CEO of Case-New Holland and current chair of the World Economic Forum USA, who said, "I always focused on being happy in what I was doing. If I was motivated and did my job well, I knew the money would follow." Rosso's not alone. Again, from *True North*:

- Ann Moore, CEO of Time, Inc., took a low-level job at Time because she loved magazines. In spite of student loans, she pursued her passion. Nobody in her graduating class could figure out why she would accept that offer from the many others she had, but 25 years later at the reunion they understood.
- Donna Dubinsky, CEO of Palm, worked at Apple Computer for half of what she could have earned elsewhere because she loved technology and figuring out how to make computing tools more accessible.
- Howard Schultz, founder of Starbucks, left a high-paying gig at Xerox with student loans still being paid and said this: "It was like a relationship that is safe, but you're not in love."

From his book *Delivering Happiness*, Tony Hsieh, founder of Zappos.com, said:

"I made a list of the happiest periods in my life, and I realized that none of them involved money. I realized that building stuff and being creative and inventive made me happy. Connecting with a friend and talking through the entire night until the sun rose made me happy... I thought about how easily we are all brainwashed by our society and culture to stop thinking and just assume by default that more money equals more success and more happiness, when ultimately happiness is really just about enjoying life.... I didn't realize it at the time, but it was a turning point for me in my life. I had decided to stop chasing the money, and start chasing the passion."

I've found this to hold true in my own career: pursue what you love to do and do it well and the money will follow. The trick is that it takes time and patience and a healthy dose of trust and belief – belief that if you do what you love, even if it doesn't pay a fortune, it will eventually pay off in both happiness and money.

Society expects you to take the most money you can as soon as possible. Sometimes this makes sense, like when you have significant debt to pay off. But over the long-term the principle holds true. Happiness leads to success and money. Money never leads to happiness, but may relieve the burdens that get in the way of happiness, at least up to $75,000.

In the meantime, whether you make that much or not, I have found from personal experience that living according to certain principles, many of which are presented in this book, can help you manage the "burdens" that can get in the way of happiness, leading to well-being. And, of course, the sooner you find what you love to do and start doing it the happier you will be (and, I believe the money will come because you are doing what you love).

As I mentioned at the beginning, what I've learned and implemented over the past 10 years may or may not make you millions but it will more than meet your needs.

Chapter 3 Reflection

How does money relate to your idea of success? Where does it rank among your values?

Try the exercise mentioned in the chapter. If you were to list out all the stuff you need money for each month in order to be adequately happy, how much would you need?

How much money would you need in order to get by at a minimum? In other words, what's the low-end of the range?

"Money has never made man happy, nor will it, there is nothing in its nature to produce happiness. The more of it one has the more one wants." –Benjamin Franklin

4. THE FOUNDATION OF YOUR RESET

After nine months pitching gas remedies, I did it. I pulled the trigger and quit. My wife gave me the nod that she would follow me into the darkness, my dad gave me confidence that I could do it, my buddy Colin thought I was insane, and I put in my notice at The Firm that I was leaving. Because I knew they would need a reason and "my Inner Voice told me to" sounds crazy, I made up a story about going back to school to get an advanced degree in Spanish.

I had no intention of doing that, but it's what everyone else needed to hear. I wasn't even confident enough yet to publicly embrace the seminary dream, but that was ok. I knew where I was headed. Note that naysayers and even passive indifferents need reasons. They have to know why. Supporters just nod their heads and say, "You can do it, whatever it is."

My wife and I picked a city in Utah, just outside of Salt Lake City, because we had friends there. My buddy TJ found us an apartment which we rented sight unseen, we loaded the Penske truck, and we headed off to figure out my career – my wife, our one-month old daughter, Halle, and me.

This is the part where others say "and the rest is history." That's the problem with most books about career. I want to unpack the "history," give you some structures, and provide you with real-life stories – my own and others – that will paint a picture for how to get from the Penske truck to the career you want.

First, in order to figure out what you really want to do, you have to let go of some pre-conceived notions that might be holding you back. They held me back for years. In my experience as a career coach, I've found that there are three myths that come up over and over again:

Myth 1: Career is linear, or in other words, where I think I will be in 10 years is exactly where I will end up.

If you think about this for a second, the probability is totally unrealistic. Twelve years ago today I was kneeling on a tile floor in Puerto Rico installing an alarm system as a technician for an alarm company. I never could have imagined where I would be now because this career path was not part of my reality. A lot can happen in 12 years, and to land precisely where you thought you would a decade or so from now would mean that you have total control over the universe around you and any element that could potentially shake you from your path.

I was talking with a friend awhile back who said that her goal was to get a job in 6-8 years at IDEO, an innovation and design firm in California. She had seen a video about them at the beginning of her college career and loved the environment they fostered and so she would end up there. The plan upon arriving to Rice was to study mechanical engineering for four years, get into Stanford, complete her master's in two years, and get a job at IDEO. I asked her how the plan was progressing and she admitted it was a little shaky. Imagine that.

The challenge with this strategy of identifying a goal on the distant horizon and heading toward it is that 1) you may find upon arrival that it's not what you thought it was, 2) you could very likely get re-routed along the way and end up in a quarter-life crisis, and 3) so much of this plan is outside of your control.

You can't make decisions on behalf of Stanford, the master's program, or IDEO, nor do you know if a job will even be available when it's your time! Very few people seem to end up where they thought they would be, and that's largely because career isn't linear. It's a nonlinear, dynamic process of self-discovery where each step ideally leads you closer to living authentically and contributing your strengths to the world to benefit humankind. Note the word "dynamic" as in not static and stale. Change is good and is often the only way to get us closer to who we want to be and how we want to live.

So take it one step at a time. She did, and she landed at General Electric working on innovative projects while using her degree in engineering to make a difference.

Should you have a long-term vision? Yes. But only a vision. Not every step. It only works to take career one decision at a time. Any further in the future and you're planning things that are simply out of your control. Additionally, vision should be focused on who you will be and what you will do, not who you will work for.

By the way, the worst question you can ask a college student, or for that matter anyone who is exploring career, is "what are you going to do with that major when you graduate" or "what are you going to do five years from now?" Five years ago my current job didn't exist and when I was in college there was no major in leadership development.

Myth 2: There is *one* best-fit job.

I have never seen this more clearly than during my time working for universities. Students come into college with the mindset that they have three choices: medical school, graduate school, or consulting and only one of them is the "right" choice. Law school may be in there for a few of them, but generally speaking most students matriculate and graduate with the same mindset.

Most students don't even realize there are thousands of firms and agencies hiring for all kinds of jobs if you are willing to do the legwork to find them. Granted, we're preconditioned to think this way in college because there are a predetermined number of majors, say 32 or so, and we're supposed to fit into one of them. The result is that you graduate believing there are also a finite number of jobs that fit neatly into those 32 majors. Then, when you realize there are 32 billion different jobs you panic and default to what you know. For me, again, this was public relations.

My first career test was in high school, and it predicted that I would end up in horticulture. I can't see many connections to what I do now other than that I spend my days helping humans grow and I like to eat horticultured things...like bacon. So what happened? Well, the majority of career inventories set out to discover who you are and place you in a best-fit profession. The challenge is that once you arrive you will likely find that each profession is run by a variety of skill-sets that aren't exclusive to that industry.

For example, virtually every business on the planet needs an accountant, someone who is good with managing systems, a leader of people, a strategist, human resources, and the list goes on. I would posit that a more effective way to begin to look at career is to decide what roles align with your strengths, and then to narrow down industries based on your values, or the causes that drive you. In other words, there are many places you could fit in the world, the goal is to find the ones that allow you to be the most of who you are.

Myth 3: "That industry definitely isn't for me."

This phrase is most often used in conjunction with careers in counseling, teaching, and non-profit work, and usually this is because we have a tendency to discount entire industries based on limited information and misguided paradigms.

What's a paradigm? It's simply a pattern of thinking. In other words, you have "patterns of thinking" or natural biases about various jobs and careers that may be (read: likely are) inaccurate.

When I was in college I considered a major in psychology. I took a class in it and really enjoyed it. But then I got to thinking that if I graduated in psychology I would have to be a counselor, and I couldn't bear the thought of dealing with people's personal problems day in and day out. So I bailed on the major based on limited information and my pre-existing perception. Ironically, I now spend my days working with people through their career problems and helping them be better leaders – and I love it.

This concept happens all the time in my career conversations with people. I've met with several students who have a talent-set that would make them excellent educators. When I say "educators" did you think "teacher" as in "high school" or "college?" It turns out every industry in the modern economy employs educators but we may call them by different names: marketers, brand experts, sales staff, etc. At their core, these individuals educate.

Typically the knee-jerk reaction when I say "You would be a great educator" is a panicked look of doom. For the record, I'm an educator in the purest sense, as in a teacher, and I love it and find it to be a noble and satisfying career. But the idea that we foreclose options based on our paradigm of what they are gets us in a world of trouble. Lawyers don't necessarily chase ambulances, psychologists aren't necessarily counselors, IT people do more than program (maybe), and educators exists in places other than institutions of learning.

We also make broad generalizations about industries because "I once had a really bad teacher" or "my friend worked at a non-profit and survived on Ramen" or "my parents say you can't make a living in teaching." The reality is, as previously stated, every industry needs a multitude of skill-sets to make it run, and "there's always room at the top of any industry for those who love what they do."

Universities are notorious for underpaying their employees, and yet there is someone at most private universities making a million bucks a year to manage the university's investment portfolio and endowment. This person probably didn't go into investment banking dreaming of working at a university, but had they discounted that option they may have missed out on the many other benefits that come with working on a college campus.

So if career is non-linear, there is no one job for me, and my perceptions are skewed, how do I choose a major or career?

Choosing a career is really about narrowing down options based on what you *do* know instead of what you don't. Much like that nifty AutoTrader.com commercial where the cars are being filtered through the character's brain stem, your goal is to filter out options that you know won't be a good fit based on what you know. And, just like the commercial, the information you need to know to figure out your career is mostly within you already...you just need to mine it out with some directed reflection and by asking the right questions.

If you narrow the target you are aiming for you won't feel so overwhelmed. So what do you know that could help in this process? What information could be most helpful in getting closer to a best-fit career path? Let me start with what not to do.

Outside/In, Inside/Out

From what I have observed over the past 10 years, there are really two ways to go about choosing your career path: the Outside/In Model or the Inside/Out Model (trademark pending for the super creative names).

Most people choose this one:

Outside/In Model

With the Outside/In Model, you begin your career search by looking at all of the options "out there" and then cramming yourself into the one that most peaks your interest.

From the 200+ individuals I've interviewed, the consensus is that most people choose a major or career based on at least one of the following:

- My dad was a _____ so I will be too (as if career is consistently passed through the blood line).
- XYZ career path pays really well so I'll do that.
- XYZ major only takes _____ credits to graduate. Let's do this!
- I really liked studying the Renaissance in high school, so I'll be a History major.

- I loved Mr. Jones, my high school math teacher. He changed my life. I'll be a math major.
- My parents are paying for my schooling and they said, "We're not paying for you to go to ABC school to get a degree in that!"

In other words, when people choose a major or career path they typically follow a relatively arbitrary and ineffective model of looking at all of the options they perceive to be available and then fitting themselves into one of them, much like fitting a round peg into a square hole. A graduating college senior might say, "Well, I can go into teaching, consulting, or pursue graduate school," pick one, and go with it. I did this when I graduated and most of the individuals I career coach do a similar thing.

The First Step to Beano

When I was in college, I visited with a career advisor. We'll call him "Doug." I felt like he would be my seer, easily identifying what it was that I was supposed to be doing with my life.

I set up an appointment and gathered my thoughts about what I love to do. I went to the Career Services office and was surprised to see how empty it was. Everyone else must have figured out their careers already.

After a brief and basic introduction, Doug asked me what my major was. I had seven majors in my brief two years enrolled in college. English was my first instinct out of high school because I could speak it fairly fluently. I quickly changed to Psychology which lasted one class period – I slipped out of the over-sized lecture hall after hearing the longest string of unrecognizable words and made a beeline for the Add/Drop screen on the Library computers. There was a brief foray into Humanities, Spanish, and Sociology. Business felt too cutthroat. At present, I had landed in Communications because, well, I enjoyed communicating.

Doug was going to take me deeper. Doug had been helping college students peer into the depths of their souls for years and undoubtedly had a wealth of insights. He would help me pick the major that would change my life forever.

"What do you like about Communications?" he asked.

"The people. Definitely communicating with people. I'm good with people," I said.

"Can you...relate...well with them?"

"I think so...yes."

"So you can relate well with people...with the 'public,'" he asked.

"Sure," I said.

"Public relations."

And just like that, in 30 minutes, I found my life's work. I would be a public relations practitioner.

Two years later I would graduate and become the Beano man. When I graduated with a degree in public relations my first Google search was for "jobs" in "public relations" in "Dallas." Likewise, when I initially selected my major I chose it based on super limited information. In hindsight, this process was broken for so many reasons, most of which fall into the Three Myths above.

Instead of searching for a career based on limited information and perspective, start with what you do know – yourself. I call this model the Inside/Out approach to selecting a career path.

Inside/Out Model

First, spend significant time answering the question "Who am I?" That's a complex question to answer and most people struggle to answer it because it's huge. I prefer to break it down into three distinct areas:

1. What do I care about? (Values)
2. What do I do best? (Talents)
3. Where do I thrive? (Environment)

Based on the answers to those three questions, you would then use that internal information as a lens through which you can sort the myriad options that are "out there" in the world. Filter the results through your new lens and ask yourself, "Does this position align with what I know about myself? Does it allow me to be who I am?" You then narrow your options to eliminate the jobs that you know ahead of time are going to cause internal conflict or handcuff your strengths and consider the jobs that are most likely to set you up for success. By taking a proactive approach, you are also taking ownership of your career path.

By the way, this is where another person acting as a sort of career coach, asking the right questions and taking notes, can be invaluable. If you share your honest goals, values, talents, and environmental success factors with another person, be they partner or mentor, they can help you identify positions that will allow you to thrive and they can help you spot potential problem areas with positions that might prevent you from thriving.

Using the Inside/Out approach has three distinct benefits:

1. You increase the likelihood that you will gain satisfaction and energy from your field of choice. By predetermining that the conditions of the job align with who you are, you set yourself up for satisfaction.

During the interview for my last job, my future boss asked me if I had any questions for her. I essentially took out my notes on what I knew about myself and phrased that knowledge as questions. "How much opportunity will I have to teach concepts to people who choose to come to our programs to learn about them vs. people who are forced to be there? Will I have opportunities to retool existing programs? How much of my day will be spent engaging with people? Is there flexibility to innovate and take the programs in a new direction?" When I realized that this job would yield massive energy because it would allow me to be who I already was 85% of the time I knew I would be able to bring my best self to work every day and essentially get paid to be me.

2. You increase your success rate because you are basing your decision on information that is concrete, that is, information that you know to be true about yourself based on past experience. In the past I have thrived coaching people one-on-one. I have a mind for it and they generally walk away feeling like they've improved or gained new insight and direction. So if I find a career that allows me to do that daily, the chances that my employer will recognize me for what I do well shoot through the roof! Suddenly people will be applauding you for a job well done when all you are really doing is what you have historically done well 99% of the time. Use what you know to set yourself up for success in a career that lets you be you.

3. You potentially increase your earning potential depending on the marketability of your skills. It's my hypothesis that when you base your career on happiness and valuable service instead of money, the money follows naturally because you are doing what you love and you become better at it than those who are doing it just because. With time you hit a tipping point when the market recognizes your greatness and pays you to be you. Happiness and financial success become intertwined in an upward progression. For years as I was toiling away and making a median salary I questioned if that tipping point would ever occur. I'm here today to say that it does happen, although it takes time. You reap what you sow, and sometimes those seeds take some time to sprout.

On the next page is a chart to summarize the concepts:

Outside/In Method to Finding Your Vocation (aka What We All Do)

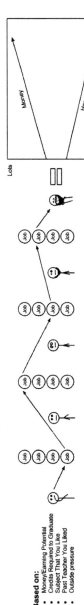

Based on:
- Money/Earning Potential
- Credits Required to Graduate
- Subject That You Like
- Past Teacher You Liked
- Outside pressure

Why this is lame:
1. Takes time. Lots of time.
2. Options limited by what you don't know you don't know. Ya know?
3. Pre-existing paradigms about fields. "You mean all psychologists don't listen to people's problems?"

Inside/Out Method to Finding Your Vocation (aka Harder Yet More Rewarding)

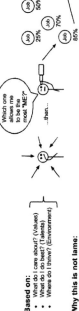

Which one allows me to be the most "ME?"

...then...

Based on:
- What do I care about? (Values)
- What do I do best? (Talents)
- Where do I thrive? (Environment)

Why this is not lame:
1. More satisfaction/energy at the outset
2. Higher success rate
3. Potentially more $ depending on market demand for your skills

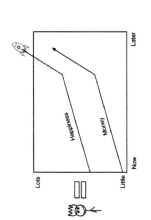

Do Inside and Out

The key to this whole Inside/Out Model is that you do what I call the Inner Work and the Outer Work concurrently. Outer Work includes expanding your paradigm of what exists in the world by researching potential just-right jobs and discovering options you may not have known existed. Inner Work consists of developing self-awareness to help you filter through the options and choose the one that allows you to be most congruent.

If you only do the Outer Work of researching ideal jobs you are shooting blind. You will ping pong around with nothing to guide your search. Like a ship with no rudder, you'll end up wherever the opportunities take you, whether they fit well with your inner self or not.

If you only invest in the Inner Work of self-reflection and getting clear about who you are you run the risk of becoming extremely self-aware and being no further along than when you started. Not only this, but when people discover the power of self-awareness, they swing on the pendulum from being robotic doers to being empowered by self-knowledge. The tendency then is to become almost addicted to building more self-knowledge which has the potential to breed discontent in your job and life as the disconnect between who you are and what you do on a daily basis grows. You become like a captain of a ship at dock, always planning and charting and mapping and never setting sail. The key to finding balance is to act. Learning who you are is only powerful in that it provides a lens through which to take action.

A friend of mine first started learning who he was but

quickly became discouraged by that self-knowledge because the gap widened between his work and his authentic self. The only thing that brought him out of that place was to begin to merge what he does with who he is. This process of connecting your authentic self to your daily work is the real key!

Because we all typically default to the Outer Work, I propose starting with the Inner Work: clarify who you are so that you have a lens to begin filtering options. Over the next few chapters I'll lead you through this process.

A Word about Authenticity

This is it. This is where the real work begins. You've got to get clear about who you are so that you can aim that self-knowledge in the right direction and capitalize on what you do best. Knowing who you are and living congruent to it is called authenticity and it is essential for success in career. For any of the exercises in the rest of this book to do you any good, you have to be willing to be honest with yourself. Remember, nobody's going to read this but you unless you share it with them. So allow yourself to think whatever you really think without judgment or worry about what anybody else would say. Just be you.

5. THE ONE THING YOU'RE NOT DOING

During a business trip a few years ago, I met with Dr. David Abshire, the President and CEO of the Center for the Study of the Presidency and Congress in Washington D.C.

Dr. Abshire has lived a successful life in policy and government and has done many important things that I couldn't begin to summarize or even understand. In fact, he's held a different title for every year of life I've lived. Whenever I meet with successful people like him, I pay special attention to the advice they have to give. Whatever helped them get to where they are may aid me in my journey too. At the end of our meeting, my colleague asked the Doc one of my favorite questions: "What piece of advice would you give to someone who is just starting out in his or her career?"

I shouldn't have been surprised by his answer – it is the same thing I teach time and again to individuals I work with who are trying to figure out what to do with their lives. It is also the core of being a great leader. In other words, it is transcendent wisdom that can be applied to virtually anyone and is the key to figuring out how to live a life of meaning and joy.

He stated simply, "It's like Socrates said: 'Know thyself.' Run recon on yourself and figure out what you're good at and what you're not. Then do what you're good at and hire someone else to do what you're not good at." In other words, take some time to intentionally analyze yourself and seek intel about your strengths and weaknesses – run recon. Simple as that. And yet, knowing yourself is not all that simple; in fact, it takes a great deal of work.

Figuring out your life path requires you to do some things that seem to have lost traction in the past two decades: stop and think. We have to stop what we're doing long enough to analyze why we are doing what we're doing, how it makes us feel, and who we are becoming by doing it. In our fast-paced culture, this is uncommon. We are taught that "time is money" and it seems that time spent reflecting is time that could otherwise be invested in working at some trade. The process of identifying your passion is an investment. The more effort you put into reflecting in the front-end the higher the payout as you give your full energy to a vocation you have intentionally identified.

Knowing yourself comes as a result of consistent self-reflection, and reflection takes effort. Self-reflection is more than allowing fleeting thoughts to materialize and then fly out of your mind as quickly as they appear. It requires you to actively think about your day and the experiences you had through the lens of a specific question or set of questions. As with military recon, the more in-depth the "intel," the more effective the strategy for a successful campaign will be. Let me explain.

Doing What You Love

It's important to understand at the outset that when people tell you to "just do what you love" they are both right and wrong. Yes, you should pursue something you love because you are more invested in things you love and you get more return on your investment. Think puppies. Or your family. But they may be wrong in suggesting that if you love singing you should be a singer. Or if you love basketball you should head for the NBA.

I made the mistake of charting a course to a career in professional basketball that ended when I was 14 and got cut in tryouts. I didn't get far. All my life when people suggested I should just do what I love for a living I poo-pooed them, feeling like I had missed my calling in basketball and was forever doomed to just work out the rest of my days in job purgatory. "Well, if I failed at doing what I love I guess I should fall back into line with the day laborers." Then, one day in 2008, I had a revelation that changed the way I pursue what I love to do:

When you ask yourself, "Well, what do I love to do?" I think you are asking the wrong question. Instead, try asking, "What do I love about what I love to do?" Say what?! Here's what I mean:

I love basketball and yet I can't do that for a career. But one day seven years ago I looked at it differently and instead asked, "What do I love *about* basketball?" Through some serious guided reflection I came up with this list:

- Working with a group toward a common goal (winning) vs. working alone.
- The strategy of working in a dynamic (constantly changing) environment to achieve a goal.
- The communication that takes place on the court, both verbal and nonverbal.
- The instant gratification of scoring vs. delayed reward.
- The use of intuition to see the court and envision how it could shift in the next few seconds.
- The competitiveness, winning, and the affirmation that comes with winning.
- Finding connections between teammates during the game that result in success – that whole synergy thing.
- Being better than other people at the same activity.
- Encouraging others and motivating them to be better.

The concept is clear. Basketball isn't what I really love. The act of putting an orange ball through an orange rim doesn't yield energy in and of itself. It's the other elements of the activity that drive the energy and joy. When I looked at what I loved about basketball and what I love about my current job it's the same. Here's how it fits:

- Working with a group – Working with a team to create leadership programming for individuals.
- Strategy in an ever-changing, dynamic environment – Predicting the needs of my target audience (a dynamic audience) and strategizing to be most effective.
- Communication – Training, teaching, and coaching one-on-one.
- Instant gratification – Watching over the course of a 30-minute session as someone "gets it."
- Connectedness – Finding connections between seemingly disparate ideas to help a client discover their leadership style or career path.
- Envisioning future trends – Creating a 3-5 year vision for the department.
- Competitiveness – Being better at my job than my predecessor.
- Affirmation – Clients thanking me for helping them change their lives.

This was mind-blowing to me and I haven't looked at what I love to do the same ever since. I don't generally love things for the sake of loving them, I love them because of what they allow me to do. Basketball is the manifestation of my talent and passion, not the talent and passion itself!

Doing what you love is not a "do-or-die" proposition. If you love to sing, you don't have to be a professional singer and if you love numbers you're not destined to be an accountant. Anyone can do what they love most of the time if they look at what they love and ask **what they love about it** and then do more of that wherever they are. Identify the transferables and transfer them to every activity you do. If I do any of the above bullets as a husband or father or Sunday School teacher or t-ball coach I feel the same satisfaction as if I were on the court dunking on someone's head or working my job!

It's a powerful principle.

After you've spent some time figuring out why you love what you love you'll find that your potential industries and career paths are blown wide open. Everything's an option as long as you can do what you love to do within its structure.

This all starts with self-reflection, and the result is self-awareness, and self-awareness leads to effectiveness in life, leadership, and career. So what should you look for? How should you begin to reflect each day? Start by taking five minutes at the end of each day to answer the following:

1) What did I do today that gave me energy? Why do I think it gave me energy? What about the situation was energizing?
2) What did I do today that sucked my life from me? Why was it a soul-sucker?
3) What do these things say about who I am? Or, what could I take away from these experiences to either replicate or avoid tomorrow in order to increase my energy and decrease my exhaustion?

Stop now and do it. Answer these three questions:

1)

2)

3)

This habit is the foundation of discovering your best-fit career. Daily self-analysis helps you clarify when you're at your best and when you're not. The more you begin amassing self-knowledge, the more clearly you'll begin to see your options.

Knowing yourself is significantly more complex than we give it credit for. It's the process of creating a profile of who you are, knowing what you care about, what you do better than others, and where you work best. It's knowing what gives you energy and drains you, with whom you work best, and what your natural tendencies are. Once you begin consistently reflecting, you need a way to organize the information. Enter the *Profile of Self.*

Your Profile of Self: The Three Things You Absolutely Have to Know

Almost any job description you read, whether on Monster.com, Indeed.com, or on a company's website, commonly contains three essential components: who they are looking for, what they need an employee to be able to do, and where they will be working and under what conditions.

Your next step is to begin to craft your personal profile which should include the same three key insights: who you are, what you do well, and where you do it best. The goal is to become so clear about who you are that you are easily able to identify opportunities that fit with who you are and those that are likely to drain your soul. Structure it like this:

Values: Under this heading, note the things you care about. These are your "drivers" or the "why" behind what you do.

Talents: This is what you do well. These are often skill-based but can come from three camps: what you think, feel, or do. We use these all the time and have been for years. Paradoxically, that's what makes them hard to identify.

Ideal Environment: This includes both physical and non-physical attributes. These may be things like "I do my best work in a shared office space with frequent interruption" or more intangibles such as "I like to work on teams" or "I thrive in a supportive environment."

The idea is to start the profile and add to it over time. As you become more clear about who you are your profile will become more powerful and energizing. Use it to weigh decisions, identify opportunities, or rejuvenate yourself when you're in crisis mode or feeling inauthentic.

Your profile can be a really powerful source of authenticity and energy and great reminder of who you are, what you do best, and where you thrive. Over the next few chapters, I'll walk you through how to develop your own Profile of Self, complete with an example at the end of Chapter 8.

Chapter 5 Reflection

Think of the activities you love to do. What *about them* do you love?

Take an initial stab at identifying the following:

Values (what you care about):

Talents (what you do best):

Environments (where you thrive):

6. WHAT DO YOU CARE ABOUT?

"Your beliefs become your thoughts,
Your thoughts become your words,
Your words become your actions,
Your actions become your habits,
Your habits become your values,
Your values become your destiny."
— Mahatma Gandhi

Too often, we are unable to identify what is really important to us. We don't live our lives in alignment with our values and then wonder why we feel unbalanced or things aren't working. Values are the beliefs that drive us on a daily basis, literally the things you "value."

The three things you absolutely need to know – values, talents, and ideal environment – are listed in that order for a specific reason: they are in order of flexibility. In other words, if you find a career that aligns with your values and talents you can alter your environment to produce more energy. Environment is the most malleable.

By contrast, if you land a job that aligns with your values and is the ideal working environment but that does not capitalize on your talents you can still alter the landscape enough to begin using your talents more but it is much more difficult. You would essentially need to begin to re-shape the core job responsibilities to allow you to do more of what you do best. Although not as easy as environment, you can control how much and when you use your talents.

Values on the other hand are tough to change. If you join an organization that simply values things you don't believe in you will never likely change their values. You also won't sacrifice your own. There is no flexibility and, eventually, the values-rub will cause you to either sacrifice who you are in your core or leave. Most people who feel dissatisfaction in their current job feel it because there is a values-rub at the core of their work – the role or organization values something they don't. Thus, the first step is to align yourself with a life's work that values what you value.

In leader-speak, we like to cram these complex values into neat one-word packages like "respect" or "empowerment" or "humility," but values are often much more intricate than that. You can represent them through a word or a statement, but they gain the most power when you describe them with a sentence or paragraph, since "belief" or "spirituality" can mean different things to different people. What they really represent is the makeup of your core.

In career, values are where you aim your talents. In other

words, values define the type of work you want to do, the organization you want to do it in, and the audience you want to do it for.

For example, I'm a developer of people. All people. I'll develop anyone, or so I thought. It turns out that when I'm developing people toward the value of "profitability" I'm de-motivated. But when I'm developing them toward the value of "maximizing potential" I'm energized. The talents and skills I use are the same, but the purpose is different. Values are all about purpose – about the "why" behind what we do. If values are misaligned, it doesn't matter what talents or skills you are using on a day-to-day basis – values misalignment = energy drain.

I'll give you a few approaches to use when identifying your values.

Approach 1: Decisions

Here's the easiest way to identify your values: think about the decisions you made over the last 48 hours. Every decision you made, large and small, had a value at its root. For example, this morning I hit the snooze and elected to sleep instead of going for a run. I value both rest and exercise, and yet, at least for this morning, I prioritized sleep over rest. If I look at the pattern over time, which value wins out? Your core values are the beliefs that consistently drive your decisions over time. Literally every decision is driven by a value. My rush to get to work on time? Timeliness. Coaching a staff member? Empowering others to be their best. Shutting down my phone to play with my kids? Responsibility to family. Turning my phone back on during family time? Competition (Madden 2013 on my phone. Lame, I know). Simply make a list of the decisions you've made, large and small, and begin to extract the values.

Approach 2: Fulfillment

The past holds the key to satisfaction in the future. Think back to a time when you felt the most fulfilled. Remember, fulfillment isn't the same as happiness. Fulfillment is a deeper feeling that all is well. Fulfillment is directly linked with meaning. What about that experience yielded meaning in your life? Why did you feel fulfilled? The answer is likely a value, and the value is usually the last few words. For example, I might say that the time that was most fulfilling for me was when I was teaching people as a missionary for my Church *because* every day I had the opportunity to help people improve their lives. There it is: help people improve their lives.

Approach 3: The Golden Question

Another way to identify values is to ask the question, "If I could do anything and money was no object and I was free from the expectations of others, what would I do every day?"

I recently asked this question to my brother-in-law who is heading down a business management path but isn't sure what he wants to do. After reflecting for a moment, he said, "I would probably be on a river teaching others to kayak." This is the part where most people would laugh and say,

"Wouldn't we all…!" or "Well, you can't make any money doing that!" But the key is to take it one step further and follow-up by asking, "What about that attracts you or draws you to that job?" For him, it might be empowering others with knowledge, teaching a skill, being outdoors, working with people, participating in physical activities, or some other value. What we love to do reflects a lot about what we care about (our values). Drill down to the core of what drives you and then use that information as a lens through which you consider opportunities.

Perhaps he becomes a kayak instructor, perhaps not. But, as I shared with him, the actual kayak and paddle probably isn't what gives him energy. It's a deeper factor. And if he can identify it he can find opportunities that tap that same value and replicate the energy it gives him.

Values change over time, but you likely have several that are more core to who you are. These are the ones that can provide direction to your career. You have to align your career with your values. When you don't, you end up pitching Beano.

Here are some of my core values that are essential for career:

- **Balance** – A desire to have a structured schedule that allowed equal parts family time, work, and personal time.
- **Empowerment** – Helping others, especially the underdog, to thrive.
- **Freedom** – Flexibility to choose my own direction, whether on a day-to-day basis or more big picture.

- **Relationships** – Opportunities to build deep, ongoing relationships with others.
- **Spirituality** – Connection to God and to others on a deep and sacred level.
- **Affirmation** – Being in an environment where I feel appreciated and others express gratitude and praise for who I am and what I do.
- **Growth** – Potential to constantly improve and develop

These values define who I am, and the key for me was to find a career that shared, or at least supported, them. You've got to learn to activate your values. There is a difference between working in an environment that respects your values and an environment that allows you to activate them. Let me give an example: I may care deeply about integrity and work in an environment that respects integrity but I may not get the same energy as I would activating integrity and working in a place that actually has me proactively encouraging integrity. It's the difference between working at a bank and being a judge. One respects integrity, the other proclaims and defends it!

Also notice that I didn't leave my values as one-word answers. The goal is to unpack them. Different words mean different things for different people. Identify your values then define them. They'll provide true clarity as you begin to define your ideal career path.

A good starting place for figuring out values is to reflect on the questions asked above. There's also a helpful activity called the "Values Grid." You can find space to work on these in the workbook pages for this chapter. If you need further clarification or another example, check out the case study below to see how values impact career.

Case Study

I spoke with a friend named Mark at church awhile back who gave a great example of how he subconsciously went through this process before landing in his current vocation as an oral surgeon. I asked him to tell me about the moment when he realized he wanted to reconstruct faces and teeth. He laughed and shared this story.

Mark went into the Air Force and drifted around from position to position trying to find what fit. He was initially driven by a desire to love what he did but after several years became frustrated and decided that he would simply find something he could do well and "work to live." He allowed the military to place him wherever they wanted and they put him in a position that worked with the missile program. It didn't take long, his wife says, before he came home and said, "I guess I actually do need to at least enjoy what I'm doing." He promptly re-initiated his search for a fulfilling career but began to pursue it in a different way.

He explained to me that he thought through a list of variables that he took into account to identify his ideal career. Subconsciously, they began with his values, which were to make enough money to allow him and his family to live comfortably and to allow him more free time in his non-work life. As he states, "I called my wife on the way home from work one day and asked her how the church party was and who was there. She said it went well and as she listed off the men who were in attendance. I realized they all had one thing in common – they were all dentists.

This is when I began to think, 'Man, I should be a dentist.'"

Aside from **flexibility** and **financial freedom**, Mark added that his younger brother had a cleft palate when he was born and, after seeing how surgeons were able to help him and repair his palate, he felt like he would like to be a part of some industry that allowed him to **serve people** in that way. Mark then noted that he also realized early on that he needed to be in a **product-oriented** sector. He said he had worked in security for some time in the military where if nothing happened by the end of the day you had done your job, and felt like he wanted a more **tangible output**. Dentistry would allow him to create tangible change each day. It also didn't hurt that Mark enjoyed **studying** and **working hard**, and as he's gotten deeper into his subject area his interest has continued to grow. He joined the oral surgery program and has never looked back. The career path aligns well with his values and will create the flexibility he desires to either work for the private sector or strike out on his own.

I asked Mark how he was able to reach this level of self-awareness and he said you have to learn how to "step outside of yourself" and look objectively at what you really like to do, that you can do well in, and what you don't enjoy doing. Too often we focus on our weaknesses and improving those areas that are deficient, but when it comes to career searching you have to focus on what you do naturally well, your strengths, and make sure your decision revolves around them. What a great way to summarize the process!

Reflecting on this conversation you can see the values emerge at the root of Mark's career search. He may not have realized it at the time but he had subconsciously began to filter out career options by beginning with his values – the beliefs he prioritized in his search: financial freedom, flexibility of schedule to spend more time with family and religion, serving others, producing tangible change on a frequent basis, and working hard. Through that lens, he likely could have chosen any number of careers that would meet those needs, but he fell into one that also aligned with his strengths and ideal working conditions. I really believe it isn't until one can identify and articulate his or her values that they will be able to narrow down their search for a career that aligns with those values.

As we finished our conversation Mark shared with me a career-related quote from Robert Frost's "Two Tramps in Mud Time" that had always driven him. He told me that he was closer to the realization of these words in his own life than he had ever been and it felt incredible:

> "But yield who will to their separation,
> My object in living is to unite
> My avocation and my vocation
> As my two eyes make one in sight.
> Only where love and need are one,
> And the work is play for mortal stakes,
> Is the deed ever really done
> For Heaven and the future's sakes."

"Two Tramps in Mud Time"
-Robert Frost

Discovering Your Highest Values

Too often, we are unable to identify what is really important for us, we don't live our lives in alignment with our values and then wonder why we feel unbalanced or things aren't working. Use this activity to discover your highest values.

Instructions:
1. Choose your top ten values.
2. In any order, write one of your values at the top of each column in the table on the next page.
3. In the same order write each of your values at the beginning of each row in the table.
4. Now compare the values appearing across the top and along the side of your table. Write the value that is most important to you out of the two, then move on to another cell and continue the process. Work through each row until all of the boxes are full.
5. Count the number of times each value is written into the boxes of the table. The value appearing most often in this table is your highest value.

Accomplishment	Equality	Justice	Results-oriented
Accountability	Excellence	Knowledge	Safety
Accuracy	Fairness	Leadership	Satisfying others
Adventure	Faith	Love, Romance	Security
Beauty	Faithfulness	Loyalty	Self-reliance
Calm	Flair	Meaning	Self-thinking
Challenge	Freedom	Merit	Service
Change	Friendship	Money	Simplicity
Cleanliness	Fun	Openness	Skill
Collaboration	Global view	Patriotism	Speed
Commitment	Good will	Peace	Spirituality
Communication	Goodness	Perfection	Stability
Community	Gratitude	Personal Growth	Standardization
Competence	Hard work	Pleasure	Status
Competition	Harmony	Power	Strength
Connection	Honesty	Practicality	Success
Cooperation	Honor	Preservation	Systemization
Coordination	Improvement	Privacy	Teamwork
Creativity	Independence	Progress	Timeliness
Decisiveness	Individuality	Prosperity	Tolerance
Democracy	Inner peace	Punctuality	Tradition
Discipline	Innovation	Quality of work	Trust
Discovery	Integrity	Reliability	Truth
Diversity	Intensity	Resourcefulness	Unity
Efficiency	Joy	Responsiveness	Wisdom

									Values

Chapter 6 Reflection

What were your highest three values:

What do they mean to you (one sentence each)?

What careers have you explored that align with your core values? What jobs have you worked that misalign?

7. WHAT DO YOU DO BEST?

"Use the talents you possess, for the
woods would be quiet if no birds sang
except the best." – Unknown

During my time at Rice, I interviewed more than 80
people each year for a competitive summer fellowship and I
started with one simple question: What's your greatest
strength?

Answer it now in your mind. Was it easy to answer?
Difficult?

The answers I got were consistent in one way – they
were consistently vague and often lacked confidence.

"I'm good with people." "I'm organized." "I'm a hard
worker." Good with what people? Organized in what way?
Hard working in what areas? With whom? To what end?
And how does any of this make you different than the other
79 candidates?

I got to the point that I would preemptively limit

candidates' options to really challenge them to think by asking, "Other than your work ethic, people skills, and organizational ability, what would you say is your greatest strength?" Few people know the answer to this question. What's more interesting is that the answer to this question unlocks a world of self-knowledge that can help you decide what to do with your life.

Talents are the foundation of a strong career. If you can identify 6-8 things that you do naturally well and that yield high energy, and then build your career around those talents, you are essentially putting yourself in a position to succeed. Your probability of thriving is huge, and "there's always room at the top for those who love what they do." Loving what you do starts with putting yourself in a position to do what you do best.

Talents are like your fingerprint. They're unique to you. They differentiate you from the other 7.3 billion people in the world. They are your competitive advantage. And yet, too often, we neglect our talents to instead play it safe and play by the rules. We explore job opportunities as if we are robots, narrowing our options to a select few: grad school, law school, dentistry, medicine, consulting, and maybe accounting. We then get into one of these positions, look at the job description, and squeeze ourselves into it, trying to fit the mold and not create waves.

Instead, your job description should be *what* you do and your talents should be *how* you do it. Talents are the engine that drives you and the method to the madness.

According to the Gallup organization, only 17% of us have our talents in play on a daily basis. That's terrifying.

Devastating. That means the other 83% of us go days at a time without doing what we do best. It's no wonder that 80% of the American workforce is either disengaged or actively disengaged from their work (Dale Carnegie Training, "Engaging Employees: What Drives Employee Engagement and Why It Matters."). Disengaged workers are checked out and running at half steam. This is how I was in the latter part of my work at the PR firm.

Actively disengaged workers are actually trying their best *not* to work. They are the ones who don't change the water cooler and play World of Warcraft when they could be working.

The key to becoming part of the 17%, which by the way correlates with my dad's anecdote about those who end up at the top, is to figure out your talents and build your life around them. Let me show you how.

Three Kinds

Discovering your talents starts with understanding that talents take various forms. According to Marcus Buckingham and his group at Gallup, talents can be consistent patterns of behavior, thought, or feeling. Behavior seems to be the easiest to recognize. When you see Kobe Bryant fluidly dunk a basketball or Ussain Bolt fly around the track effortlessly it's simple to pinpoint talent. Think of great artists, dancers, and musicians. And yet, we often don't recognize in ourselves or others inherent talents that take another form: feelings or patterns of thinking.

Feeling talents focus on the way you sense a room or how others are feeling, or the way you connect with or move other people to action through emotion. Thinking talents are about the way we analyze, organize, catalogue, or differentiate information. Behaving talents may also be the way you organize, communicate, alter, or interact with objects or people.

Identifying Talents

The key is to look for consistent patterns in your life in either behavior, thought, or feeling. The way you act, think, and feel is not only unique to you but may actually be an inherent talent, waiting to be developed. When coaching people to articulate their talents, I usually follow a process that starts with this question:

What is one thing you have done this week that has given you energy? Something that you lost yourself in?

Energy is that rush of joy you feel when you do something that comes naturally to you. You lose yourself in whatever it is you are doing and feel whole or complete as a result. Whatever you're engaged in comes easily and fluidly without much thought. It's that feeling that you are at your best. And afterward you often feel a deep sense of satisfaction as if some need was fulfilled. These are the environmental cues that often attend energy, and energy is the key to identifying what you do naturally well.

Why is energy associated with talents? According to neuroscience, talents are developed at a very young age and manifest as highways in our brains across which brain impulses travel. Because these pathways are large and developed the transmissions flow easily, releasing a feeling of fluidity and associated endorphins into our systems. These endorphins then manifest as energy boosts that make us want to do more of whatever it is we were doing.

In contrast, weaknesses manifest as dirt roads in our brains. Small, tight pathways across which signals don't easily travel. The result is that we feel tired, weak, and sluggish, and find those activities difficult to do. An example for me is doing almost anything with Excel. Although I may have technical skills in organizing spreadsheets, the task drains my energy because it does not come naturally to me to organize data sets.

So, the goal is to spend as much time as possible on the highways that release energy. How do you do it?

First, recognize that in each moment of each day you are doing one of two things: you are either making a deposit in your energy account or you are making a withdrawal. Most of us make more withdrawals than deposits, which in the world of finance is referred to as a deficit. Because we are running energy deficits, we walk around looking drained, feel wiped out when we get home, and don't look forward to the next day. We're in a modern energy crisis.

The next step is to pay attention to those moments when you get lost in activity and analyze them. Ask yourself what you're doing and why you think it's so invigorating. A client I worked with gave the following anecdote:

"One day, sitting in on a presentation given by a senior partner, I realized that the elements of the PowerPoint unfolding before me that were of greatest interest to me were hardly the points relevant to the organization's work. I was obsessing over the design of the logos, the branding, and the slogans. Suddenly, I was consuming articles, books, and information on the advertising industry at a faster pace and with a greater ease than I had ever experienced in an academic subject."

The organization or business itself wasn't what gave her energy, but rather the way the work was communicated or delivered through advertising vehicles such as logos. Given this, she could likely find satisfaction in a job at any organization in any industry and still capture that same level of energy as long as she could work with the advertising methods. Remember, the goal is to look at activities that give you energy and mine out what about that activity is the catalyst. If you can figure out the formula for releasing your energy then you can replicate it in other facets of your life.

Now take whatever general statement you've come up with and narrow it down. Don't leave it general! "I love working with people" won't get you anywhere. What people? For what purpose? Why? And working with them to do what?

Take your time. With each question, replace a variable in the statement until you narrow down or isolate the specific, formulaic statement that is guaranteed to yield energy time and again. Once you've got it down to bare bones, to it's most raw and descriptive state, write it down. Let me take you through an example from my own experience. To be most effective, I'll take you back to my first inkling of the talent in 2008 and walk you through how I discovered it, honed it, and now apply it.

Example

I discovered a talent at UNLV in the fall of 2008 during a professional development training that I've built my entire career around. I walked out of the training having had this "aha!" moment where I accepted that **I loved to present to people**. Sharing this with others was liberating and I felt truly authentic owning up to it. I also felt a little anxious, since I hadn't explored it since my seminary teaching days in college. I was afraid I would now be held to some standard of teaching that I may not actually be able to live up to. But overall it was invigorating.

Shortly after I discovered this talent, I was asked to speak at a conference for student athletes in Georgia and was given the topic of "ethical leadership." I didn't know much about ethical leadership, but I liked speaking and teaching and they were going to pay all my expenses and give me some extra cash. I liked cash. So I took the gig. Standing in front of that group of athletes a few months later I felt my soul leaving my eyes. I couldn't stand it. I felt totally drained afterward and couldn't wait to get out of town. On the flight home I had an identity crisis. Why is it that I felt drained after doing what I do best – teaching?!

Studying talents further, I figured it out. I hadn't been specific enough. I dove deeper and decided that I loved to teach topics I was interested in and for people who wanted to listen. Not only was I not real interested in ethical leadership (sounds weird, I know) but the group was forced to be there. And it was the night of the Super Bowl. I started getting a little choosier with the gigs I would do. I also began to narrow my niche areas. What I really loved was career, authenticity, and self-awareness.

The key is to get specific about what you do best.

Talents Aren't Strengths

Now that we've explored talents, let's go a step further. Talents alone are not enough to be successful in identifying and thriving in a career. According to Marcus Buckingham and the Gallup organization in *Now, Discover Your Strengths*, the goal is to turn raw talent into strength. Strengths are defined by this formula:

Raw talent + knowledge + skill = Strength

Raw talent is the stuff that makes up who we are, those natural and instinctual things you do better than most others intuitively. Knowledge can be either factual or experiential. Factual knowledge comes from books, classes, lectures, research, etc. Experiential knowledge comes when you put your hand on a hot stove and decide to never do that again. Skills are transferable. They are things you can teach someone else to do. Mowing the lawn, cleaning a paint brush, operating Excel, bathing a dog, completing a TPS report – these are skills.

We often confuse the manifestation of talent for talent itself. For example, the other day I attended a conference where I listened to a really passionate and dynamic public speaker. The temptation would be to walk away from that experience and say, "Wow, that guy was a talented public speaker." In reality, "public speaking" isn't the talent. The talent was his ability to articulate and transfer passion and energy into words. The knowledge was education reform as well as knowledge from books and past experience about what makes a great speech. The skills were eye contact, voice inflection, hand gestures, PowerPoint, and a well-constructed speech. When the three combined, he became a strong public speaker. He could probably take that talent – articulating and transferring passion and energy into words – and deploy it in many situations such as a coaching session, a check-in, a team meeting, or convincing his contractor to lower his price. But unless he adds knowledge and skill his raw talent remains just that – raw.

Most of us are surviving on raw talent. Think LeBron James when he first entered the NBA. All that guy did was dunk on folks. Eventually, he began adding knowledge and skill to diversify his game and redirect his talent for fluid athleticism, court vision, and sharp instincts (among others). The result is that he has become one of the games most prolific defenders, scorers, rebounders, and team leaders. He's taken raw talent and developed it. We each have the opportunity to do the same.

Talents are part of the raw building material each of us has at our disposal to create our best work experience. The key is to identify them, develop them, and build your work around them.

Utilizing Talents

If we are empowered to do what we do naturally, utilizing our innate gifts and abilities, and if we are given opportunities to develop those qualities, we will maximize our potential and be more productive. Like the principle of the "path of least resistance," which states that objects (or in this case people) will follow the path that provides the least resistance to forward motion among a set of alternative paths, humans are more likely to do what is natural than to invest effort and energy into unnatural or uncomfortable things.

Unfortunately, society values individuals who are "well-rounded" or "jacks-of-all-trades." We configure our resumes, our training, and even our personal lives around developing areas of weakness. We invest significant time in self-development efforts that focus on taking what we don't do well and trying to turn the tide, so to speak. The self-help industry has made a fortune off of "one-size-fits-all" training programs and generalizations that state if you organize your life in this way or if you improve your life in that way then you will finally be successful.

I, myself, have struggled to introduce complex organization systems and scheduling into my daily ritual that have resulted in great frustration and an almost adverse effect. I have listened to self-help books and read about concepts that seem to propose a "silver bullet" solution to rather complex dilemmas, such as managing people, making more money, speaking in public, and developing relationships. I have spent a great deal of time trying to make connections between these things to develop in my mind the makeup of the ideal human so that I could then invest myself in becoming more like that person. I have felt discouraged and tired.

I have even rebelled much like the out-of-shape individual who tries to embrace a new, generalized workout plan, and then quits shortly thereafter because the plan doesn't feel natural or isn't returning the expected results. There is a reason that personal trainers exist – they learn a person's strengths, body type, and goals and then customize a plan to get them where they want to go. Eventually, the person learns enough to chart their own course. The same is true for personal finance consultants.

What I am suggesting is that the power lies within each of us to be our own consultant. You and I can learn enough about who we are, what motivates us, and our own nature and tendencies to then develop a plan to get to where we want to go. In fact, it is essential to achieving joy!

Neglecting this process will lead to further discouragement and aimless wandering. More importantly, turning your back on your identity, or minimizing the need to explore "self" only postpones the inevitable soul-searching.

I was recently talking to a client who summed up his strengths journey like this:

> "You go through life either being good at things or not. You feel like you need to be good at everything and so you constantly figure out how to improve your weak areas. But now I see that I have specific things – talents and characteristics – that are unique to me.

Identifying those and developing them will help me be more efficient. It will help me free up time because I'm doing what I do best and what is most important. I can home in on the things I really need to focus on and push aside the things that matter less."

As I shared with him, the whole goal of strengths and talents is to move closer and closer to them in your day-to-day work until you are getting paid to be you – paid to wake up in the morning and go to work and do what you do best. Anything else you bring is, as I said in the Introduction, just icing on the cake. Instead of excelling because you pour a lot of time into work, you're excelling because you are who you are.

Here is a list of some of my talents:

- Using my competitive edge and talents to take something that is good and make it better than it was before I got to it.
- Synthesizing information for individuals that is important to their development.
- Preparing a lesson with good questions about something relevant to me and for people who want to listen.
- Facilitating and teaching something I care about for an audience that wants to listen and that benefits their life.
- Researching information about a topic that is interesting to me and that I can use to benefit others.

- Adding value in a way others may not be able to either due to lack of skill, knowledge, or experience.
- Observing a method for solving a problem or dilemma and then replicate the method, improving it or enhancing it to make it better.

The goal is for your statements to be general enough to apply in many situations but specific enough to really tap into the energy. So what do you do best? Take some time to figure it out in the workbook page following this chapter.

Case Study

I recently worked with a student to help him identify his natural talents and aptitudes. I started by asking what I usually ask, which is "what do you enjoy doing?"

He said he enjoys solving problem sets for his engineering class. Taken at face value, that doesn't separate him from the other thousands of engineering students at Rice or really any other university. So we explored further. I asked what about solving problem sets gave him energy. He got more specific and said that he enjoyed working through the process of imagining an outcome and then working toward it.

This is the beginning of true self-reflection. Many students can solve problem sets, but each will do it in a different way. We were beginning to get down to his natural talent with problem sets, so I pressed forward with additional questions such as "tell me about your process." In the end, here's what we came up with compared with where we started:

Student's initial statement: I like solving problem sets.

Student's refined and reflective statement: I like taking a complex problem and using my ability to visualize in my mind the finished outcome, and then to backtrack that solution into smaller, more manageable steps that I can then follow to work toward a solution.

When we arrived at that statement and I read it back to him, the proverbial light bulb came on. He lit up and said, "That's exactly what I do well!" It was as if he was discovering this about himself for the first time, even though he always knew it.

Once he identified it, he was able to think of numerous other times when he had used that same natural talent in various contexts to arrive at a solution. In fact, this same talent that helped him achieve success in engineering problems is exactly what he utilized in his hobby building bikes.

The epilogue to this experience is that he had an interview with an engineering firm several days later for an internship. After the interview, he came into my office beaming and told me that the company had asked during his phone interview what his strengths were. When most students would have said something to the effect of "I like solving problems" he was able to say very specifically what it was that he did – and how he did it – and to cite multiple examples of times when he had done it. Needless to say, the company was impressed with his self-awareness and offered him an on-site interview that resulted in a paid internship offer.

Talent is the core of a best-fit career. Take some time on the next page to reflect on what you do best.

Chapter 7 Reflection

Think back to last week. When did you feel most energized?
Describe that moment below:

Now look at the raw data and develop a statement that
summarizes the thing you were doing that gave you energy –
it may have been a way of behaving, thinking, or feeling:

Now simplify it even more by taking that statement and refining it with questions like, "Does it matter who I do it for" or "why was I doing it" or "what the topic was"?

Finally, write that statement in a concise way that captures the energy but is general enough to be widely applicable:

Use this space to explore other natural talents. The goal is to identify 6-8.

8. WHERE DO YOU THRIVE?

Picture a moment in your life when you thrived. Better yet, picture a moment in your future when you are happy and thriving. Get the image in your mind. Now turn in your mind 360 degrees. Look around. Who's there? Where are you? What are you doing? What's in the environment? What about the space makes you happy and fulfilled? Who are you interacting with and how are you interacting?

The vision you have in your mind yields major clues from your inner self about the type of environment that is most fulfilling. Environment includes physical space, emotional space, schedule, travel, and any other structural component that influences the way you work. Environment is about "where you thrive" and is important because it can determine whether you're able to activate your values and utilize your talents in a way that is fulfilling.

Environment is one of the most underrated factors of career exploration and yet it holds great power. I can be doing something that I love to do, say career coaching, but if I'm doing it in a dingy, windowless office on someone else's time and strictly over the phone then the talent loses all power to yield energy. Where you thrive is just as important as what you are doing and why you are doing it.

One of the best ways to identify the type of environment you might thrive in is through a personality or behavioral assessment such as the Myers-Briggs Type Indicator (MBTI). The MBTI can tell you whether you would prefer an environment that is more extroverted (E) or introverted (I), more big-picture focused (N) or detail-oriented (S), more focused on human impact and values (F) or on analytical and objective reasoning (T), or more organized and methodical (J) or flexible and spontaneous (P).

The assessment is my go-to resource for figuring out ideal environment and is backed up by loads of research from people smarter than me. That said, you can still learn much about your ideal environment through some simple introspection. Following the case study is an example of a reflection activity you could do.

Case Study

Recently, I was career coaching a colleague to help her better understand the role environment can play in her satisfaction at work. In fact, taking control of your environment is one of the easiest and most tangible ways to boost your joy in the workplace!

We worked through the questions at the beginning of the chapter and she decided that her thriving moment was in college. I asked her to look around 360 degrees and tell me what she observed. Here's what she said:

- I'm in my sorority house.
- The room is buzzing.
- Everyone is in their "family" groups or teams.
- There is a sense of urgency.
- Everyone seems to know what they're doing and has a clear picture of what they're working towards.
- Blinds are shut so no one sees in.
- It's only the girls that I really know and love.

As she talked, I took down these notes and then we went back one-by-one and explored each with the simplest, most profound question: Why? Why is each component there?

- It's in my sorority house. Why? This was the last time in my life when happiness wasn't gray. I knew exactly in that moment that that was where I was supposed to be. (I had certainty). I was a leader. It felt like a good fit. People saw me as vital to the group's cohesiveness. (I felt needed). I was doing a job others had done poorly in the past. (I was improving something ineffective).
- Buzzing. I love being around people. I love the energy of lots of people being around. (People-oriented).
- Everyone's in their "family" groups or teams. I had orchestrated the camaraderie and group work. I value collaborating. Love seeing the girls who didn't

normally interact interacting. They're all over the place – some on floor, working together on the couch, some at tables. (Varied workspace? People work with what they have and find creative uses for their space.)

- Sense of urgency. I like people working together with a plan or goal in mind. I'm not competitive, but I love the energy in the room. Everyone was happy and that seemed to exemplify itself in the urgency.
- Everyone seems to know what they're doing and have a clear picture of what they're working towards. I get motivated by working around people who know what they're doing or are dedicated to what they do. That's why I chose the people I studied with. Why I like working in here. I like being around people who have figured out how to like their job.
- Blinds are shut so no one sees in. Like feeling a part of something special. (Like to be in on things).
- It's only girls that I really know and love. (I value deep relationships).

After understanding why each aspect was a part of her ideal environment, we boiled down these factors into simple statements. It became clear that she would work best in an environment with these characteristics:

- Certainty – clarity about expectations
- Feels needed – has a skillset that is valuable

- Improving something – working to make something good, better
- People-oriented – lots of people around
- Varied workspace – opportunity for creative uses of the workspace and the resources
- Competition or urgency – Working with others toward a goal with a sense of urgency
- Competence – like-minded people with competence in their area and who are infinite thinkers
- "In" – strong and deep relationships that make her feel included and "in" on things
- Inclusive – making others feel included and a part of the team

Note the connection to values. There is definitely some overlap and many values represented. That said, there are also some purely environmental factors at play, such as a varied workspace and people-orientation.

A few weeks after we had this conversation, several of us left for the week and she was alone in the office for a few days. Upon returning, she said, "At first I didn't believe in environment, but it makes all the difference!" While we were out, she found herself alone in a static workspace and felt totally drained. By simply varying her workspace and working in a high traffic area with other colleagues she instantly boosted her energy. She has continued to put herself in a place to succeed by clarifying expectations, seeking to add value, working in a space surrounded by colleagues, and changing up her workspace.

Below are some of the environmental elements that put

me in a place to do my best work:

- Lots of natural light and open space
- Frequent interaction with others
- Opportunity for distraction – working on multiple projects at once
- Job that allows for big picture thinking
- Collaborative work
- Travel during the workday – no one consistent workspace
- Flexible time for unexpected family occurrences

Remember this: If talents are what you do best and values are what you care about, environment is where you most thrive.

The Inner Work is all about getting clear about who you are. Your inner self is the lens that you can use to look at potential majors, careers, or opportunities and screen out ahead of time those that are incongruent with who you know yourself to be. Alas, if all you do is Inner Work, you'll become really self-aware and be no further toward achieving your vision. Ladies and gentlemen, up next is the Outer Work.

Chapter 8 Reflection

Think about a moment when you thrived. Now, in your mind, turn 360 degrees and picture the environment. Remember, pay attention to both material and immaterial factors. Material factors might include actual office space and surroundings. Immaterial factors might include job expectations, travel, and amount of interaction with others. Describe or draw your ideal environment below:

PROFILE OF SELF

At this point, if you've played along you've developed the core of a Profile of Self. Below is how I've chosen to format my profile:

Profile of Self

The Why for My Existence: I exist to show people the best in who they are and help them actualize their potential.

My Profile:

Values

- Balance -- A desire to have a structured schedule that allowed equal parts family time, work, and personal time.
- Empowerment -- Helping others, especially the underdog, to thrive.
- Freedom -- Flexibility to choose my own direction, whether on a day-to-day basis or more big picture.
- Relationships -- Opportunities to build deep, ongoing relationships with others.
- Spirituality -- Connection to God and to others on a deep and sacred level.
- Affirmation -- Being in an environment where I feel appreciated and others express gratitude and praise for who I am and what I do.
- Growth -- Potential to constantly improve and develop

Strengths

I feel strong when...

- I help individuals synthesize information that is important to their development.
- I prepare a lesson with good questions about something relevant to me and for people who want to listen.
- I facilitate and teach something I care about for an audience that wants to listen and that benefits their life.
- I research information about a topic that is interesting to me and that I can use to benefit others.
- I can add value in a way others may not be able to either due to lack of skill, knowledge, or experience.
- I can observe a method for solving a problem or dilemma and then replicate the method, improving it or enhancing it to make it better.
- I can use my competitive edge and talents to take something that is good and make it better than it was before I got to it.

Environment

- Frequent interaction with others
- Opportunity for distraction -- working on multiple projects at once
- Job that allows for big picture thinking
- Collaborative work space
- Travel during the workday -- no one consistent workspace
- Flexible time for unexpected family occurrences

MBTI: ENFP

- E: I get energy from people, externalizing ideas, being interested in many things, and working on many things at once. Remind me when you need time to process.
- N: I'm big picture, futuristic, and love ideas and theory. I see the whole event as one big picture in mind instead of a list of linear actions or steps to get there. Help me figure out the steps or process.
- F: I make decision by how people will be affected, how they will feel about the decision, and who will be impacted and in what way. Help me see the logical side of decisions we make.
- P: I'm spontaneous and flexible and open to change. This also means I may not come across as organized and I do my best work last minute (the day before and day of). You need to press me for answers and give me deadlines.

Formatting is less important than content. It's all about capturing this info in one place that you can consistently turn to in order to stay true to yourself in decision-making. Of course, the profile is no good without options. Let's figure out how to generate options.

9. THREE KEYS TO OUTER WORK

As you're clarifying who you are you should simultaneously be investing significant time in the Outer Work. In fact, this is where you actually create opportunities to do what you do best. Step one of getting a job you love is actually the easiest part – get a job. It almost doesn't matter what job. Just get something to start with. You're better off having some employment while you figure this out than no employment at all. Plus, nothing helps you clarify your values like being in a job that reinforces some values and rubs others.

Remember, the goal of the Inside/Out Model is to begin clarifying where you fit best by understanding yourself while also expanding your understanding of what careers are out there and what they realistically entail. This is most easily done if you can remove the stress of money by working *any* job.

If I could go back and do it all over again, I would spend my time doing three things: 1) Being Exceptionally

119

Curious, 2) Building a Constellation, and 3) Strategically Collecting Experiences.

Let me explain each.

1) Be Exceptionally Curious

Being curious is about doing three things – practicing the habit of exploration, broadening your paradigms, and looking to the top. Before you can effectively develop this habit you've got to have a genuine curiosity to learn about others.

Practice the Habit of Exploration

When I decided public relations wasn't for me but I didn't know what was, I began to practice what I now call a "habit of exploration." This strategy was *the* game changer. I would not be where I am today had I not been practicing this habit every chance I got.

After quitting my job and moving to Utah, I secured a job as a customer service representative at Overstock.com (again, just get a job. Any job). This job served several purposes: 1) It provided an income; 2) It felt mind-numbing and therefore drove me to earnestly seek a new profession; 3) It was simple and allowed me to store up enough energy and brainpower to spend my non-work hours vigorously exploring potential life-paths.

In fact, I made a habit of informally interviewing every individual I could. I would generally ask some variation of the following questions:

- What do you do for a living?
- What does that actually mean?
- How did you decide you wanted to do that?
- What do you like about what you?

The results of these conversations were fascinating and led to two very distinct outcomes: 1) They broadened my perspective of what was "out there" career-wise, and 2) I realized, and this is significant, that I was not alone. A jarring result of my dialogues was learning that virtually no one was content in their field. Many people did not feel like they were doing what they loved and an even greater number had no clue what they really wanted to do. In fact, they would often turn the questions back on me, to which I would reply:

- I answer phones.
- I quite literally mean that I answer phones.
- I'm only doing it for the paycheck and to buy me time to figure out something else.
- I like nothing about what I do. Actually, I like that it provides me with an alternative to the Tomb of Rejection. There's something less-threatening, almost soothing, about a 70-year-old woman complaining about a broken chair or a misplaced order of duvet covers. Anything is better than a bitter journalist griping me out for asking them to cover flatulence in the next issue of *Your Body Quarterly*.

This "habit of exploration" was really a key to unlocking my future career path. In fact, it was while engaging in one of these conversations that I discovered the path that led me to teaching leadership at the university level and conducting training for companies and non-profit groups.

I was chatting one day with my close friend, Matt, and asked him what he was going to do when he graduated. He said he was going to go into Higher Education and Student Affairs Administration. What? What is that? He explained that he would get paid to work with college students and develop programs to help them grow and progress. I worked through the four questions and felt this immense rush of energy. I knew enough at this point to pay attention to my Inner Voice and explore it more, which put me on the path to where I am today.

The goal, then, with self-exploration and vocational searching is to take a rather wide spectrum of potential career paths, ranging from gardener to astro-physicist, and begin to reduce the options by filtering them through what you know to be your strengths. The end product is a fairly narrow range of possible paths, any of which will allow you to maximize your potential and all of which will yield a high degree of success and satisfaction. This all starts by having a better understanding of these career paths, and practicing the Habit of Exploration will get you there.

Broaden Your Paradigms

By "broadening your paradigms" I mean that you have to remove the mental walls that constrain what you believe a job to be. The truth is, you may have an idea of what you think a job is like, but you haven't experienced it yourself. Being open to what you hear from those in the field is an important part of understanding whether a job or industry will be the right fit for you. Throughout this process, you'll undoubtedly come across job titles that sound like they're just what you want, but upon further inspection, you will discover that they are really not what you imagined.

Most people I've worked with as a career coach believe they have a limited number of options. We are all guilty of this to a certain extent. The opportunities seem so limited. And yet, there are literally millions of different kinds of jobs in almost as many industries. The only way to find out what exists is to do your research.

Peruse job boards and keep your ears open for interesting jobs, and when you hear about one Google it. Every time I come across a blogger, author, speaker, or leadership educator, I Google them and read as much as I can about who they are, how they got there, and why they chose it. Notice that you've seen those questions before.

This strategy shouldn't take the place of the next one because it lacks a crucial, personalized last step which is recommendations and suggestions, but it's a great way to bust paradigms and become more knowledgeable about what's out there.

Look to the Top

As we discussed earlier, "there is room at the top for those who love what they do." One of the best strategies for figuring out what you want to do and how to get there is to identify people in the world who are doing exactly what you want to do (at least as you perceive it) at the top of their industry and then set up opportunities to learn four things from them:

1. Why did they choose that career path? What were they hoping to get from it and what was their motivation?
2. How did they get there? What steps did they take? Did they pursue certain degrees or certifications?
3. What do they actually do all day? What does their job look like? Highs and lows?
4. What recommendations would they have for someone wanting to be just like them one day?

Question 1 is really geared toward figuring out if what motivated them aligns with what motivates you. For example, if you are wanting to get into investment banking to make a pile of money and you talk with someone in the industry who got into it to help corporations thrive, you may hear a new perspective that causes you to realize that your values may not align with the industry.

Question 2 is about pathway. The answer will give you a roadmap with concrete steps that you could follow. This will build your confidence.

Question 3 is a clarifier. Being a doctor and actually being a doctor may be two different things. This goes back to the Inside/Out Model and our incorrect paradigms about what the day-to-day jobs actually are. Being a doctor on TV is about heroic heart transplants, ER politics, and relationships outside of work. Really being a doctor may or may not include these things but it also likely includes paperwork, meetings, and a lot of downtime waiting for emergencies or sleeping on cots between shifts while on call.

Question 4 will give you your immediate next steps. Your goal should be to get tangible action steps. This is also the place where you should ask for a referral – a recommendation of someone else like them who you may benefit from learning from using the same four questions. Keep the momentum going!

When I decided I was interested in pursuing a career in higher education and student affairs I set up an informational interview with the VP of Student Affairs at the University of Utah. She was a mentor of Matt and he helped me get a 30-minute meeting. It changed my life. In this meeting I asked these four questions and found serious alignment between who she was and what she was doing and what I wanted to do one day. I walked out with a list of six grad schools I should apply to (one of which I ended up attending) and I dropped her name as a contact several times during my interviews at the various schools which built my credibility (with her permission).

This strategy is money for a few reasons. First, you discover that career isn't linear. Rather, most people get to where they are by simply taking opportunities as they come and winding their way through experiences until they land in something that fits who they are. As we talked about earlier, it's one decision at a time. Also, you learn that getting to where they are is *very* possible. It doesn't seem so distant or impossible to achieve.

There is at least one other benefit. You will begin building a great network. Inevitably, as you show sincere interest in learning about others – especially those in positions of power – they will turn their attention on you and ask what your interests are. It's human nature. They will be curious about you and that will oftentimes turn into a mentoring relationship or some other opportunity. Of course, you shouldn't go into these conversations expecting that and you especially shouldn't be expecting or gunning for a job offer. People can sense hidden agendas and ulterior motives. But by building the connections you will begin building a network in the very industries that most align with who you are.

One word of caution: Because the law of reciprocity will kick-in and people will turn the conversation to learn more about you, you should be as prepared as possible to answer the question, "What do you want to do?" The key is to do the Inner Work. Figure out your values, talents, and ideal environment. You don't need to answer with a specific job, and you may not want to say "I want to be you" because that may be creepy, but you will want to be able to say, "I'm not sure, but I know what I am good at and it is _____, _____, and _____. And I was drawn to interview you because you do _____ and _____ and the environment seems like a good fit."

Again, this strategy is one of the best and easiest. It

works even better if you find people doing what you would love to do *at the top of the industry.* If I could do it all over again I would have spent significant time interviewing people who I perceived to have "made it."

One last thought here. You may wonder, "How do I go about getting a conversation with someone?" Using your network is always best, but you can also cold-email someone to introduce yourself and share your intentions. Whether you have a connection or not, you should always preview the conversation so that the other person is clear on the outcome. Your email might follow an outline like this:

- I'm exploring career options.
- I would like to seek insight on four questions. (list the four)
- Below is some brief background about me.
- Express gratitude and looking forward to it!

Anytime you can meet in person it will be to your benefit, unless you are extremely weird. Phone call is second best. A back-and-forth email conversation is the worst, but still beneficial. Again, preview the conversation so that you can maximize the time and get what you most need – a glimpse into "a day in the life."

2) Build Your Constellation

My good friend came up with the term "constellation" as a way to avoid saying the word "network" but the concept is the same. One of the greatest ways to magnify your Outer Work efforts is to begin to track your contacts in a constellation of sorts. Keeping track of who you know, what they do, and where they do it can be huge. And, remember, when you invest in relationships with others the law of reciprocity kicks in and they can't help but be interested in you.

When I started at my most recent organization, I decided pretty quickly that the best way to engrain myself into the strong organizational culture would be to get to know as many people as I could as fast as possible. I worked in the Administrative Office with about 100 other people. I set a goal to meet one new person a day.

Sometimes this was really easy and sometimes I had to awkwardly introduce myself at the water cooler or in the hallway. Immediately after meeting them I went back to my computer where I had a spreadsheet entitled "Contacts" and typed in their name, title, and any random stuff I learned about them in our conversation that I might want to remember in the future. Looking back at it I had some really random stuff in there. Bald head. Texans fan. Loud voice. I also had some really helpful stuff, but more random stuff. After a month I had 57 people in the spreadsheet. Fifty seven new contacts and allies! My strategy was never more extensive than wanting to get to know my colleagues and feel a part of the culture, but it ended up paying off in several different ways.

For example, two weeks into my new job my PowerPoint started malfunctioning. The protocol was to send an email to the HelpDesk, await a reply, turn in my laptop for a day, and wait. Instead, I pulled up my spreadsheet where I had met three IT guys during a random drop-in introduction. I refreshed my memory on their names and stopped by their office. After some chit chat, I mentioned my issue and they took my laptop straightaway, fixed it, *and* – on the hush hush and with a wink – upgraded me to the new Microsoft Office Suite before anyone else had it. Truth is, the upgrade mattered more to them than to me, but the power of the constellation was in play.

How you track your contacts is up to you. The important thing is that you track them and keep them fresh. Become a master networker. As you may have noted, I mentioned in the "Habit of Exploration" section that I was interviewing anybody who would talk to me. This was part of building my constellation. I didn't always form lasting relationships with everyone I talked to, but I did make some important contacts just through exploring the experiences of others working in the field I was interested in.

It is also important to remember that you don't have to map out your entire network before you even get started. As you start to meet people, you'll find that they also have contacts that they can refer you to. Your network will naturally grow without you having to do all of the legwork of figuring out who you need to meet.

My good friend Lindsay had this experience with building her constellation:

"I was feeling stuck and questioning whether I should even be in higher education, so I went to meet with a career counselor a few times. Initially, I thought that I might want to be a career counselor, but I was hung up on the idea that I can't call myself that without an advanced degree in counseling. After talking about what I like to do (help people tell their stories, understand why they pick the careers they do) and my reservations about not having an advanced degree in counseling specifically, she mentioned that I could consider resume writing as a vocation. It doesn't require an advanced degree and would allow me to do the things that I like to do. She put me in touch with two other resume writers in the area. I didn't even know that I needed to meet them, but I actually learned quite a lot. Just being open to possibilities outside of what you'd already considered is key."

Talk to other people and find out what and who they know.

3) Strategically Collect Experiences

Counter intuitively, this is the third strategy. This isn't because it's not important. Most articles tout this as the primary way to figure out your career path. I partially agree. Getting experience is crucial, but experience isn't enough. You've got to get the right experience. Taking on an internship or practicum, or shadowing someone for several weeks, is time intensive. And, with most internships, you may dive into a two-month commitment and know within a few weeks that it's not for you. Granted, there are still many great experiences you could have and things you could learn but you will also be locked in for two more months.

Again, I want to clarify that this step is crucial, but it is especially effective if used as a capstone step to the other strategies. If you've spent time doing the other four strategies and narrowed down some great options that you think will tap your talents and be interesting areas of growth then the best thing you can do is commit to an internship to test it out.

I will say that getting an internship in anything is better than no internship at all, but if you've taken the time to invest in the first few strategies then this step will pay huge dividends.

So how do you land an internship? There have been many books written on this topic. In the spirit of not replicating resources, let me share a few unconventional tidbits.

First, getting an internship starts before you ever even know you need one. You should be proactively getting to know many people in many industries with no expectation of a job (see strategies 1 and 2 above).

Second, you need to determine whether or not you can afford to live for a month or two with no income. If you can accept an unpaid internship the options are limitless. Almost anyone will take an unpaid intern and these will often morph into something paid. If they don't, you show significant grit by being willing to work hard for free. And, because you're not paid you're also not committed. If it's horrible, get out.

Lastly, if you want an internship but aren't sure if a formal program exists, ask! There are generally two kinds of people in this world: askers and guessers (see Andrea Donderi). Askers ask for what they want without regard to the consequences. As a result, they often get what they want.

They sometimes get rejected but, speaking from experience as someone who is married to an asker, they get some really cool stuff.

Guessers, on the other hand, only ask for things they have 95% chance of getting. They don't want to put people in the uncomfortable circumstance of having to say "no" so they only ask if they are reasonably sure the answer will be "yes." Guessers often take extra shifts from askers so that askers can have the day off. Be an "asker" when it comes to internships. The worst that can happen is that they will say "no."

There are, of course, other ways to get experience in an industry short of getting an internship. For starters, you can just do whatever it is you want to get experience in. When I wanted to get more expertise speaking and leading workshops, I volunteered at church to do more of it. As a result, a buddy at church who had seen me teach a class asked if I ever did any leadership training for organizations. "Of course I do." The reality is I had not done much but I scored a gig. The key word here is "volunteer." You may spend significant time doing unpaid work in a variety of industries but this doesn't make the experience a waste of time. Remember, the Outer Work is all about exploring what's out there.

Chapter 9 Reflection

Develop a Habit of Exploration

What are some things you want to know about the career field that you're interested in?

Who do you perceive to be at the top of your career field? What can you learn from this person's example? What was his or her path to the top?

Build Your Constellation

Who are some people you can think of off the top of your head that might be able to tell you more about the job you're considering? When could you find the time to meet with them or contact them another way?

What are some of the questions you'd like to ask people you interview?

Who can advocate for you with regard to the skills, talent, and knowledge that you'd like to use in your daily work?

Collect Experiences

What are some experiences that you've already had that have served to point you in the direction of your dream job?

What are some experiences you'd like to have? How can you be strategic about the experiences you choose?

10. WHAT NOW?

"You will be most effective as a leader when you find
opportunities that highly motivate you and utilize your
greatest capabilities."
– Bill George

Ok, now you're doing the Inner Work to determine
who you are and the Outer Work to begin to expand your
idea of what's "out there." You have your Profile of Self and
you're wondering what to do next.

The goal now is to churn up as many options and
opportunities as you can. In reality, you don't really have a
decision to make until you have an option. Many people get
stuck here. I worked with a client a few years back who
couldn't decide whether they would accept a new job or stay
put and wanted to make the decision before ever applying
for the new job. I coached her that she didn't actually have a
decision to make until she had an offer. My actual advice
was, "Just apply. If you don't get it then the decision is

made. If you do get it then you have an option. I always recommend applying – always let someone else tell you that you aren't good enough but never preemptively do it to yourself."

By the way, options aren't always a good thing. The more options you have, the more difficult it is to make a decision. In fact, more options can be overwhelming, not liberating, and lead to decision paralysis.

The easiest decision to make is whether to stay on your current trajectory or to make a leap to something else. By using your Profile of Self, you can analyze both options to determine which one will offer you more opportunity for congruence. Here's how to do that:

Take each option, one-by-one, and sort it through your Profile of Self.

First, start with values. Values are the least fluid. They don't really change, either for you or for the role/organization. Does the organization believe what you believe? Do they value the same things?

For example, when I was considering a job at Rice, I gathered from the Website and from my interview that the culture of the office was all about creativity, change, and education. I also asked questions during my interview that helped me ascertain that my boss valued work-life balance, hard work, and family (she had two kids of her own). Looking at this in connection with my values, it was a direct hit:

- Balance – A desire to have a structured schedule that allowed equal parts family time, work, and personal time.

- Empowerment – Helping others, especially the underdog, to thrive.
- Freedom – Flexibility to choose my own direction, whether on a day-to-day basis or more big picture.
- Relationships – Opportunities to build deep, ongoing relationships with others.
- Spirituality – Connection to God and to others on a deep and sacred level.
- Affirmation – Being in an environment where I feel appreciated and others express gratitude and praise for who I am and what I do.
- Growth – Potential to constantly improve and develop

Next, move on to talents. These are usually couched as "skills" or "duties/responsibilities." Here were mine from the job description:

- The Associate Director works closely with the Director to realize the vision of Leadership Rice and enhance the development opportunities Leadership Rice provides, <u>including the revision or expansion of existing programs and the introduction of new programs</u>.
- Supervise and <u>train</u> student workers
- Work with Director to administer the Summer Mentorship Experience program, including executing the application and selection process, <u>corresponding with participating students and mentors, and facilitating training course</u>

- Prepare and deliver leadership-related workshops and seminars and represent Leadership Rice at internal and external functions.

And my talents:
- "I feel strong when I facilitate and teach something I care about for an audience that wants to listen and that benefits their life."
- "I feel strong when...I can use my competitive edge and talents to take something that is good and make it better than it was before I got to it.
- "I feel strong when...I prepare a training with good questions about something relevant to me and for people who want to listen.

As I asked questions to clarify the responsibilities and the audience I would be working with it became clear to me that I would have ample opportunity to do what I love.

Finally, analyze environment. You can discover much about the environment by visiting via an onsite interview. You can also ask questions like, "Describe a typical day working with you" or "how would you describe the office culture" or even "what is the environment like for the person in this role?"

Not all things about the environment were immediately clear. I knew I controlled my opportunities for distraction. I also knew I would be in a collaborative workspace and doing some big picture thinking. I wasn't sure about travel or flexibility, but I sensed I would have opportunities to move and shake.

Compared with what I was looking for the environment was a good fit:

- Frequent interaction with others
- Opportunity for distraction – working on multiple projects at once
- Job that allows for big picture thinking
- Collaborative work space
- Travel during the workday – no one consistent workspace
- Flexible time for unexpected family occurrences

Remember, values are the least flexible and environment is the most. The goal is congruence, so as you compare the option or position you are assessing to your Profile of Self you are looking for clues that would tell you that the position aligns with who you inherently are.

Disclaimer: No role will be 100% congruent nor share all values, provide for all talents, nor do so in an ideal environment. That's not realistic. But the **core** of the job should align and allow enough autonomy and flexibility for you to carve out your niche.

Chapter 10 Reflection

Compare Your Options

List the options you are considering below. Now compare each against your Profile of Self. Which ones align most with your values? Talents? Environment?

Give each a percentage score from 1-100%. What percentage of the job is aligned with who you are?

11. DEFINE SUCCESS

"Comparison is the thief of joy." – Teddy Roosevelt

So you're doing it. You're on your way to getting paid and doing what you love. But there's still a pretty significant question you need to answer: how will you know when you've made it? What will success actually look like?

Success is a tricky thing. I remember becoming trapped in the "self-pity vortex of doom" a few years ago. When I turned 31, I found myself yet again comparing what I had accomplished to individuals who were similar in age (or younger) but who had seemingly accomplished greater feats. In fact, I spoke to a mentor on the night of my birthday about the difficulty of turning 31. He said, "I can relate. When I turned 30, I thought to myself, 'When Jesus Christ was 30 he was beginning his mortal ministry. What am I doing!?'" Granted, this may be an extreme example — I was comparing myself to Jon Bon Jovi and Mark Zuckerberg — but the concept is the same.

Back to the vortex. I began to wallow in the self-pity of what I had not yet accomplished and spiral downward into a joy-sucking cyclone of unhappiness. I had not yet written a book. I had not established a successful speaking company. I had not made a million dollars…Warren Buffet made his first million at 30. And yet I had been given so many gifts and talents that I felt could be ideally suited to being "successful."

Enter the sage. The sage is really any person in my life who shares wisdom that awakens me from my self-indulgent slumbers. In this instance, it was my friend, Judy. I shared with her my conundrum and she listened intently and with understanding. She, too, had experienced these feelings of inadequacy. From her experience, she was able to immediately diagnose the problem…how do I define success?

What a profound question. What is success? As I began to think about this, it occurred to me that what other people had that I didn't wasn't simply millions of dollars and a nice car. I am not intrinsically motivated by money — don't get me wrong, as long as I can do what I love and get paid really well to do it I won't complain.

But what really made me feel inadequate was when I saw individuals who had similar talents and abilities to my own but who seemed to able to do so much more with them, affecting large masses of individuals in a positive way. Judy said it best: "Right now you are the boutique of happiness and good will and you want to be the superstore." Dead on.

So how do you define success? Before you can ever

begin to feel the feelings of fulfillment and satisfaction that come with maximizing your potential, you have to understand your metric for success. In searching for a career, I suggest that the question to ask yourself might be some variation of "what will my life look like when I've "arrived?"

You have to articulate what you're aiming for and remind yourself of it often. I did this several years ago as I was preparing to leave grad school. I was having one of my conflicted career moments, trying to decide what I should pursue next. My friend Bob was talking with me and challenged me to distill what it was I wanted down to the most basic, pure, simplistic statement that I could. I told him I wanted to be a public speaker, encouraging audiences to live better lives and be more authentic. He helped me take it deeper, asking what I hoped would be the outcome of my speaking. We came to a simple phrase – a personal mission statement. For me, it's alive, and every time I read it I get energized. I pulled out a little yellow sticky note and wrote on it, "I want to inspire people to live up to their potential."

This sentence holds great power for me. In fact, it's guided every decision I've made in my career and it has re-energized me when I feel like I'm straying from my life's purpose. So what are you aiming for? Try to capture it in 15 words or less right now:

My purpose:

Happiness and Success

My guess is that your vision of success also contains some element of happiness. We need to get clear about the connection between success and happiness. We often see happiness as just over the horizon with success standing in our way. "If I could achieve this or that, then I would be happy." In reality, the reverse is true. Those who are happiest are most successful. We've got to flip the equation.

The problem, according to scientific research on happiness by Shawn Achor, renowned Harvard professor and author of *The Happiness Advantage*, is that each time we experience success our brain changes the bar for success. In other words, once I achieve a goal, happiness is short-lived as my mind automatically begins to explore what else could be possible. I raise the bar and begin anew, searching for more happiness by being more successful. I read my scriptures five nights a week and the goal becomes to read them seven times a week. I find a job that aligns with my strengths 80% of the time and now I need to find one that aligns 90% or 100%. Run a mile? Now run two. Score high on the GMAT? Could've been higher. If, in my mind, happiness lies just beyond success then I will never get there!

Achor says that if we can raise someone's level of positivity in the present then we increase the likelihood of success. Your brain at positive performs significantly better than your brain at negative, neutral, or stressed. In fact, your brain is 31% more productive (this is called the "happiness advantage"). In other words, we've got to take this:

$$Success = Happiness$$

And do this instead:

$$Happiness = Success$$

That said, I don't think the formula is complete even like that. I recently received a new responsibility at church with some serious scope to it. I've never felt such a steep learning curve. Shortly after receiving the responsibility, I was mowing the lawn and reflecting on how lost I felt in this position. I wasn't sure where to start or how to contribute and have the biggest impact. A quote came to mind that I had heard many years ago from Gordon B. Hinckley: "Forget yourself and get to work."

Get to work doing what? I would propose that the true merit of discovering your vocation and utilizing strengths comes from harnessing their power to benefit other people. This is not to say that you cannot or should not be compensated for using your strengths. There are many products and services that benefit others that generate income. However, I would suggest that the goal be people-driven instead of profit-driven.

I recognize that this is a values-judgment from someone in a human-oriented industry, but I truly believe that, regardless of occupation, when you prioritize others you benefit in the end. In response to friendly actions, people are frequently much nicer and much more cooperative than predicted by the self-interest model.

Earlier I proposed the following formula: happiness =

success. I want to add to that formula something that has made all the difference in my career.

Serving Others = Happiness = Success

Martin Seligman, the father of "positive psychology," conducted a study for his book *Authentic Happiness* wherein he asked his students to do two things: 1) to go out and have fun and 2) to do some act of philanthropic service and then to write about each experience in depth. The results were profound. The satisfaction that came as a result of having fun was dwarfed by the satisfaction that came from selfless service. In fact, when the act was spontaneous and benefited others, tapping into humane qualities, the entire day was improved and the satisfaction carried over into other facets of life. Says Seligman, "The exercise of kindness is a gratification, in contrast to a pleasure."

In other words, you can feel great satisfaction in dominating your competition and "winning" but that satisfaction is of the short-term kind. Lasting happiness and satisfaction lies in altruistically serving others. Note: This does not mean non-profit work, nor does it mean becoming a monk. One can serve the needs of others for profit (and lots of it!) but this could be an outcome of serving the greater good rather than an end unto itself.

Indeed, it seems that the moment we begin using gifts to attain profit we lose one of the greatest aspects of strengths – their ability to bring happiness. Remember that the whole goal of this process of discovering what makes us different and capitalizing on it is to increase satisfaction and joy, and tap into dormant potential. If you are using your strengths, the money will come because people will recognize you for your natural gifts and this will increase your marketability. People will pay you to be who you are because when you are congruent you will also be fluid, dynamic, and successful. Dave Ramsey says, "If you serve enough people, you don't have to worry about money." Moreover, science shows that undertaking an act of kindness for others leads to increased satisfaction.

Chapter 11 Reflection

Create Your Own Definition

A few years ago my wife and I tried something new — I had read about a reflection activity in *You Unstuck* by Libby Gill that helps you clarify where you're going. We buckled down and did the activity before watching a movie. In about five minutes, we had a pretty profound experience. I invite you to play along. You can either read through the entire activity or work through it step by step. It can be completed almost anywhere (e.g. in your car, in the shower, on a long run…you get the picture) and goes something like this:

Close your eyes, get comfortable, and take a few deep breaths to clear your mind. Let go of any stress. Forget what you ate for lunch, block out what you have to do for the rest of the day, and focus on the here-and-now. Now continue breathing until you feel relaxed and ready to begin.

Step One: A Mental Image

Create a mental image of the life you want to live. Consider both the personal and professional, including work, family, relationships, spiritual life, etc. Meditate on your vision until it takes shape in your mind's eye. This image in your mind should be as detailed as possible. Think "vivid." If you say to yourself "I want a nice house" then let it take shape in your mind — where is it? What does it look like? How big? What is the surrounding environment?

NOTE: What you will likely find is that negative thoughts will begin to creep in and say things like "How in the world do you plan to achieve that?" or "who do you think you are?" or even "what makes you think you deserve all that?" Acknowledge those thoughts and release them, without giving them too much energy. This was key for me in this activity. As predicted, I had several thoughts sneak in and tell me I wasn't qualified or that my vision was way out of reach. You have to get past those and just let your mind wander freely.

Take a moment and write this vision down as specifically as possible.

Step Two: The Pathway

Now imagine all of the pathways to reaching your goal. You may even picture literal pathways, like railroad tracks or highways that are leading to your vivid destination. Consider specific actions to take, feelings that you want to have at the forefront of your mind, and ways that others can support you in your journey. Write these down. If you are more visual, you may consider doing a mind-map. First, draw a circle in the middle of a blank page to represent you. Then draw branches out from the center with each part of your vision represented as a circle around the perimeter. Now write a pathway on the line connecting you to the various aspects of your vision.

Step Three: The Motivation

Lastly, focus on how you'll maintain the mental energy and momentum to keep you moving toward your goal. What has kept you motivated in the past? What past successes or activities have kept you moving in the right direction? One thing that has worked well for me is sharing my vision with someone else. This creates instant accountability. One of my favorite authors, Parker Palmer, often talks about using "circles of trust," an aspect of the Quaker religion. Take a moment and write down your motivators.

At this point, you should have a pretty detailed picture of your vision, some paths to get there, and ways to stay motivated. My wife and I did this activity together and then shared our visions with each other. This was a powerful bonding activity and I learned a great deal about my spouse. (WARNING — If you do this as a couple always let your partner go first…that way you can moderate the selfish and immature stuff on your list.) Thankfully, I let my wife go first and listened in amazement as more than half of her vision was focused on the kids and me and our well-being and happiness. I looked down at my vision, which was generally self-focused with a smattering of material possessions, a house on the beach, and a Jaguar, and instantly learned that I've got some growing to do. That said, the point of the activity isn't to feel guilt, but rather to get clear about what you want. We have spent some time over the past few years homing in on our vision as a couple and then working toward it.

This is a powerful and simple activity for leaders of organizations, parents, or individuals. If you did the activity as you read along, great job. If not, I encourage you to try it. Once you've done it, set it aside and do it again in a few days. You will find that your vision will get more clear and defined. You may also learn some things about yourself that you may not have realized. After all, each of your desires in your vision is directly tied to a personal value.

Happiness

Reflect on the idea that "Serving others = Happiness = Success." In what way can you do this? What product, service, or idea do you want to offer that will be of value and benefit to others?

12. LUCK WON'T WORK, BUT THIS WILL

Before setting out to discover what you want to do with your life, you've got to ask yourself another key question: Is it worth it? In other words, how important is it to you that you find your passion? Of course, your instant reaction will be to say that there is nothing more important. But I think most of us are less willing to figure it out than we would like to admit.

Identifying your passion and putting it to work takes serious effort and patience and sometimes a healthy does of risk-taking. If not so, everyone would figure it out. Instead, a small percentage of the population seems to be doing what they love, and these are typically the individuals who invest substantial time in the process I have described in this book.

No Clear Path

Awhile back I met with a student who was at a

crossroads. We first met to talk about career about a year ago. He was on the pre-med track and preparing himself to apply to medical school this year. As we dove deeper into the "why" of this career path, he revealed that the reason he wanted to be a doctor was because it would make for an easy jump into a health and wellness related career. He wanted credibility. His dream would be to train people to live healthier and happier lives, much like a personal trainer or a nutritionist might do. I asked the obvious, "so why don't you just do that and save the decade of medical school and tuition money?" His reasoning came down to two things that I feel many people may struggle with:

1. He had a difficult time after pursuing an expensive and prestigious Rice University education deciding if this was a legitimate career path.
2. There was no clear path.

Not all people may relate with the first statement. But the second is a key problem for many. Where do I begin? The catch is that when you're pursuing an unconventional career you have to be willing to take an unconventional path. There are no obvious routes to a vocation. In fact, many times you have to carve out your space or your niche to be able to do what you love. Hence, the risk-taking. What you do best and what the world needs may not yet be in the marketplace. This of course takes a great deal of belief.

Boyd K. Packer, an educator and Apostle in the LDS Church, said, "Somewhere in your quest for spiritual knowledge, there is that 'leap of faith,' as the philosophers call it. It is the moment when you have gone to the edge of the light and step into the darkness to discover that the way is lighted ahead for just a footstep or two." The same has been true for me in my career. Every move I have made has been a step into the darkness, only to find that the next step or two are illuminated for me, but almost never more than that.

I've been in that dark place many times when I don't know what to do next but I know what I'm doing can't be it. I lived in that space for six months in Murray, Utah while I worked at Overstock.com and researched career paths. I was in it again during the second year of my graduate program at Indiana University while I decided between a Ph.D. and going into industry. This darkness is a natural part of the process.

The trouble is that I've seen too many people in that space who can't take the ambiguity and who pull the ripcord. They can't see the path because it doesn't yet exist. Logically, then, they pursue the path that is clear and stable. I wonder what we are missing out on by not being willing to step into the darkness?

Remember, though, that stepping into the darkness doesn't mean you sit in the corner, twiddling your thumbs, and waiting for the universe to provide for you. The whole idea of stepping into the darkness means that you take action...you step! I have no idea what the future holds for my career. I also have no idea what my career holds for me next month, next week, or tomorrow. But I've learned to live in that space where I take it a day at a time, live in the moment, and step into the darkness when the time comes.

If you're going to find that unconventional career and step into the 20% of people who love what they do, you're going to have to make sacrifices, and comfort may be one of them. There's nothing comfortable about living in ambiguity and uncertainty, but for me it has been worth it each time.

I'm Just Lucky, I Guess

I remember watching Bon Jovi perform on American Idol a few years ago. After the performance, which was subpar, Ryan Seacrest interviewed Jon Bon Jovi himself and asked the perpetual question: "You guys just released an album and are touring yet again. You are so successful and have reached a whole new fan base [of young teenagers]. How do you continue to do it?" Without hesitation, JBJ launched into a typical staged answer. But what he ended with is what has stuck with me. He said, matter-of-factly, "We have found that the harder we work the luckier we get." Simple as that.

Fortune favors the bold, and the bold take action.

People tell me I'm lucky because my job is awesome. I get paid well to spend my days reading leadership and self-development research, books, and articles. I present, train, and teach what I learn to a captive audience who is generally interested to learn. I receive a good amount of positive reinforcement for my efforts, largely due to the culture of the place where I work. It really is the ultimate job.

And yet, when people tell me I'm lucky, I don't like it.

The reality is that where I am today has nothing to do with luck. It was never really "right place, right time" or that I "fell into" this career path. I took major risks to get where I am today. Big ones. I firmly believe the phrase, "Fortune favors the bold." The more bold you are in your moves, the more the universe aligns to allow you to do what you want. This is often called the "law of attraction" and it goes something like this: "like attracts like" and thus by focusing on positive or negative thoughts you can bring about positive or negative results.

This isn't new. The other day I was reading an article by Daniel Goleman in the *Harvard Business Review* called "What Makes a Leader" that said that the mood or emotional state of the leader largely dictates the mood of the entire organization. Negativity at the top breeds negativity throughout the organization. I believe the same to be true in career. Focus on what you want, make moves to put yourself in position to achieve it, and like will attract like. When people say I'm lucky, here's what lucky looks like:

- Worked hard in September 2004 hitting networking events, blasting resumes, and making connections to land a PR job at a top firm in Dallas.
- Quit my job in August 2005 with a new wife and one-month old baby to move to a random destination (shout out to Murray, Utah!) to escape family and work pressures and figure out my life path.
- Admitted and openly discussed with anyone I could that I had no idea what to do for a career;

discovered "student affairs" in the process.

- Met with VP of Student Affairs at the University of Utah to learn about the industry; she referred me to six graduate schools.
- Applied to all six schools and was accepted into three. Traveled across the country alone for three weeks to interview for assistantships which were required for full admittance.
- Selected Indiana University, enrolled, and worked hard for a 3.8 GPA; landed a good internship through sheer grit and pavement-pounding.
- Searched for jobs for months and applied/interviewed at UNLV; beat out competition for job.
- Ditto for Rice University; selected from a pool of more than 80 applicants through preparation and effort.
- "Discovered" and recruited to do my current job as the Director of Leadership Development at YES Prep Public Schools.

In other words, between 2004 and 2014, I worked diligently to put myself in the position to figure out a career path I never knew existed, never imagined I could do, and love to do every day. Each bullet represents a risk I had to take to get closer to my best-fit career.

I recently listened to a speech that affirmed the idea of investing in your work and being patient in the process. The speaker, Henry Eyring, a prominent educational administrator and former president of Ricks College, made reference to two laws of nature: the "law of diminishing returns" and the "law of increasing returns." He spoke about these laws metaphorically in reference to farming and harvesting crops. Think of their application to doing what you love as you read them.

The law of diminishing returns essentially states that we will give the most effort to harvesting crops initially and expect in return the greatest reward in relation to the amount of effort we put forth. Great effort equals great success. Think "taking a high-paying job that I may not love but it's right in front of me and has immediate reward." However, at some point, if we have harvested the early "crops" through our initial burst of effort we cannot expect that continued harvesting will yield equally great crops. In fact, despite the amount of effort we put forth the output (read: satisfaction) will continue to diminish. The returns diminish steadily over time despite the effort we may put forth. Therefore, after our initial surge, we neglect the harvest and move on.

In contrast, the law of increasing returns states that first and second efforts to harvest may yield little. We may be harvesting the early crops too soon without letting them mature. In fact, we may harvest repeatedly and put forth effort without seeing an initial return on our investment of energy. The temptation may be to cease the harvest and put our effort toward other endeavors. However, for those individuals who diligently continue to invest time and energy into the harvest, the payout is tremendous. It may not come on our own timeline or in the way we expect it to, but it will come.

Doing what you love takes sustained effort over time to realize your potential and harvest the greatest success. Too many people who I coach expect immediate reward for their investment in the Inner and Outer Work. The point isn't to take a shortcut, but rather to clarify the process.

When I embarked on my quest to figure out my life path I felt that I had reached a point where I had no other options. It was do or die, or rather "do or dislike-my-job." You may not yet be at that point, but perhaps you can relate with how I felt.

In 2005, I vividly remember driving by a man blowing leaves in my apartment complex one morning on the way to work. I stopped at the stop sign before turning onto the street and for a brief moment I sat and admired his job. I thought, "Man, what a sweet job. No direct supervision, he knows exactly what's expected, he gets to listen to music, be outside and wear sunglasses, *and* he's essentially the master of his own destiny."

In hindsight, that was probably a totally unrealistic perception of this man's job, and for all I know he felt really unfulfilled, but at that moment I would have taken almost *any* other job than the one I had at the prestigious PR firm. Are you there yet? Do you feel the burn? How ready are you to really figure this out? What price are you willing to pay?

With any major career move comes risk and with great risk comes great reward. Sometimes you have to take a massive leap to get on the right track. The key is to have what's called a promotion mindset. Heidi Halvorson and Tory Higgins wrote an article in the *Harvard Business Review* called "Do You Play to Win—or Not to Lose?" that talked about this idea.

A promotion mindset means you see your career as being about the potential for advancement, achievement and rewards. It's when you think of what you might gain if you are successful and how you might be better off. The opposite is a prevention focus, which means that you approach your career focused on not losing everything you've worked so hard for, on avoiding danger, and keeping things running smoothly. This type of focus is good for careful planning, accuracy, reliability, and thoroughness, just to name a few. But it doesn't lead to creativity, open-mindedness, and the confidence to take chances the way promotion focus does.

Commit to living with a promotion mindset! The work it takes to do what you love is worth it. You have to believe that in order to make it through the journey that it takes to figure out your life path. This isn't a popular idea in a fast-paced, here-and-now, instant gratification world. But it will pay off.

Chapter 12 Reflection

Identify some potential risks that you may or certainly will encounter in your transition.

What are you willing to give up in order to get to the meaningful career you've imagined for yourself?

What are some ways in which you can create luck or opportunity for yourself?

13. THE ENEMIES OF SUCCESS

"The more scared we are of a work or
calling, the more sure we can be that we
have to do it." – Steven Pressfield

Many of the people I coach know what they really want
to do. Deep down they've felt pulled to something specific.
Usually, figuring out their next step isn't the real dilemma. I
can relate.

I've felt this way for years. In fact, I've been writing
this book for six years. For that same amount of time I've
known I wanted to start a company focused on helping
people maximize their potential. For more than six years
I've been called to do this work. So what's stood in my way?
Why haven't I done it until now?

This is a "trillion dollar question" as my friend says.
I've spent a lot of time thinking about the answer, that thing
that kept me from my manifest destiny. It comes down to a
few things: I'm self-aware enough (because I know what my

talents and limitations are I become self-critical about those things rather than basking in the naiveté) and lacking in enough confidence that I perpetually talk myself out of things that I would otherwise be successful doing. I'll talk more about that later on. But the real obstacle that has stood in my way until now was to simply "do something." That's it. We are often our own worst enemy.

The difference between those who've made it and those who haven't is that they've done something about it. When you do something you move toward your goal, albeit slowly sometimes and with discouragement. When you do nothing you guarantee the outcome – failure. So what stopped me from doing something? Again, that's complex. As I was talking with my friend John I realized that I'm not alone and so I want to share my challenge.

Every day I get home from work, spend some time with my family, and then the moment of decision hits around 8pm. I can either head to my study and do something, anything, to further my goal, or I can sit on the couch and watch TV. I'm ashamed to say that for the past several years the couch won 99 times out of 100. The crazy thing is, that little voice in my head told me non-stop that if I really wanted to I could go to the computer and make something happen and I would likely be successful. And yet I did nothing. It's as if knowing I could be successful if I wanted to was good enough. The voice talked to me while I sat on the couch and watched TV until suddenly it would be time for bed, the voice gave up, and I decided that "tomorrow will be the day."

Distraction is one of our greatest enemies. It

prevents us from being great. And yet we willingly let it into our lives.

Likewise, John was meant to be a teacher, but more specifically a health and fitness educator. He taught cardio kickboxing classes for four years and loved it. When he taught he combined many of his strengths which yielded an immense amount of energy. People frequently commented that his class was one of the best. He thought about it all the time when he wasn't doing it. He even envisioned himself having already "made it," walking down the street and seeing people who say things like, "Hey John! I just signed up for a year of your class – can't wait!"

He loved the idea of empowering others with the knowledge they needed to take care of themselves and improve their lives. He loved the physical aspect, is a charismatic person, and loved to role model for others the steps to success. So what was he going to do when he graduated? Medical school. He was going to pour four or more years and thousands of dollars into medical school to become an MD. This is the path his parents wanted to see him take and it's a lot more conventional, structured, and secure than venturing out into the world of physical training, physical therapy, and health and fitness.

I can't blame him, particularly because the thing that stopped me for many years was precisely the same. There's value in the conventional path. And yet, as I told him, that little voice in his head – that urge – to do something with health and fitness won't go away. I promise. It stays there, pushing you and driving you toward doing what you were meant to do.

You can ignore it and press on, accumulating experiences, but eventually you will come back around to what you knew you should be doing all along. My advice to him was this: address it head on. Take it seriously. Listen to it, try it out, understand it and understand your options, interview people doing what you want to do, and then if after all you can do you decide it's not for you then move on. But don't ignore your inner self. It knows you better than your friends, parents, or society, and it knows what you are capable of.

The problem is that we think too much. It's a mental game. Perhaps it's that our brains are hard-wired for survival, but we have a tendency to self-defeat and self-select out of potentially high risk and high reward activities. I recently wrote a letter of recommendation for a student who was wanting to apply for law school. We'll call him Bryan.

Bryan took the LSAT and got a score that was just below the advertised threshold to have a chance at a top three law school. He was discouraged. He retook the test and got the same score. In spite of having all of his essays, letters of recommendation, and application materials together, Bryan decided not to apply and to take a gap year instead to work and take the LSAT again. I was discouraged because a) that letter of recommendation took a ton of time to write and b) I thought he was selling himself short.

I asked why he wouldn't just apply anyway to, say, the top 10 schools in the nation. If he applies, three things happen: 1) he opens himself up to the chance that he may be the anomaly at the top three, 2) he gets into other great schools and reconfirms his awesomeness, or 3) he gets flat out rejected by the whole world and can move on in life and never look back or recommit to working harder for next year. If he doesn't apply he gets 1) nothing. Actually what he gets is a lifetime of wondering what might have been. Now there's a chance that he could apply and decide to take none of the offers after all, and that's okay, but to foreclose an option without the option ever being there is ridiculous!

Too often we self-select out of activities that we are probably ideally-suited for and well prepared to handle. What a shame. I'm the master at this, and so can speak expertly on this topic. But I'm also here to shake you and I out of our mediocre slumber and say "wake up!" Let other people reject you, but don't ever reject yourself.

In contrast to Bryan's story, I met with another student named Juan who wanted to go to medical school. He took the MCAT and got a 29. Top schools are looking for 35s. He was very discouraged. He had an average GPA, great letters of recommendation, and good past experience. So he took it again and got...a 29. Discouraged, he decided to press forward anyway, put himself out there, and see what happened. He applied to 15 schools, 12 outside of the state and three within. He got rejected from all 12 outside the state and accepted into all three within. Not only that, but one of the schools he got accepted to has a median score of 33 on the MCAT. He interviewed there, feeling a bit fraudulent, and nailed it. And now he says that he can't imagine going anywhere else. The culture is a perfect fit and he's thrilled with his option.

Don't over-think it. Just act. Much of what has stopped

you until now may have been your own self-doubt.

Be Childlike

I think you already know what you want to do for a living. Your inner self has probably been giving you clues your whole life. But there's something standing in the way. More on this in 60 seconds.

Figuring out what you love to do is sometimes as easy as going back to the way you were when you were a kid. Remember back when you were less affected by societal pressure, you weren't yet part of the system, and expectations were low? You probably followed your passions and pursued whatever most interested you naturally. Your options were wide open.

I see it in my own kids now – my 9-year-old daughter thrives on competition and is a natural friend-maker, my 7-year-old loves the strategy behind LEGO-building and video games, my 5-year-old is creative, sensitive and empathetic to his younger brother, and my youngest is a natural athlete. They pursue their passions because they don't know any other way. Said another way, when you were a kid work and fun were opposites. Now you're trying to blend them and it's tough to do.

Eventually, my kids will get sucked deeper into school where they will be told what they should be learning – the core subjects – and then on through junior high and high school they will learn to conform and fit it. It's not cool to stand out at that age. They will head off to college to become even more specialized and then we, as a system, will kick them out in the world where options are wide open again for the first time since they were five. They won't know anything else but to find a steady job, conform, and play the game. At some point, they will feel disconnected with their jobs and begin to explore like they did when they were kids...allow themselves to dream.

Why not start now? Figuring out your passion starts with going back to a carefree, expectation-free world and asking yourself the question, "If money was no object, what would I do?"

The truth is, I believe most of us already know what to do with our lives, but what's standing in the way is some combination of fear, anxiety, misunderstanding, doubt, pressure, expectations, and the word "should."

All our lives we gather clues about the type of work that would be most rewarding, and almost cruelly, it is often a work that doesn't flow well with the "shoulds." Let me explain with a personal example:

I've always known I was meant to motivate people, to be in front of people, teaching, training, motivating, and empowering them through facilitated sessions, the written word, and any other medium. I first knew this at six years old when I was the only kid in my church Primary to memorize my lines for the Sunday Primary Program and deliver them with zest while making eye contact with the congregation and connecting with them. I knew it when I was 16 and delivered a talk from the pulpit at church and was afterward told that I had a natural talent for speaking. I knew it, ridiculous as it may sound, when I was given the "actor of the year" award in ninth grade for my performance in Chaucer's Canterbury Tales.

I knew it when I spent two years teaching the Gospel as a missionary for my church. And I especially knew it when I was asked to be a Sunday School teacher after my mission for a group of 100+ peers in my college church congregation and I prepared and delivered some killer lessons. So why, then, did I go into public relations?? Why did I flounder from 2003-2008, not knowing what I should do?! The writing was on the wall. What prevented me from diving into teaching?

At least four things stopped me, and they may be stopping you as well. We've touched on all four, but I'll review them here. First, self-doubt. As discussed earlier, I didn't think I was good enough to make it to the top regardless of my efforts.

The cruel thing about what you do best is that it may also be the thing you fear the most. You see, when you do something that you're not very good at you tend to take more risks because at the end of the day you can punt on it and say, "Well of course I failed. I'm not good at that anyway. Never was." But with things you care about, that are part of your identity, you feel more fear and self-doubt. What happens if you take the risk and fail?! What does this say about who you are??

In a recent workshop, I suggested to the audience that one clue to identifying your talents is to look for anxiety and fear. The idea is reaffirmed in the book *The War of Art*:

"Self-doubt can be an ally. This is because it serves as

an indicator of aspiration. It reflects love, love of
something we dream of doing, and desire, desire to do
it. If you find yourself asking yourself (and your
friends), 'Am I really a writer? Am I really an artist?'
chances are you are. The counterfeit innovator is wildly
self-confident. The real one is scared to death."

Now that I teach for a living, and thrive doing it, I look
back and wonder why I allowed self-doubt to paralyze me
for so long. Michael Bernard Beckwith said this:

"Ground yourself in the intention to be radically alive.
I like these words of Dr. Howard Thurman: 'Don't
worry about what the world needs. Ask yourself what
makes you come alive, and do that. Because what the
world needs is people who have come alive.' This
means that, as long as you are on the planet, you are
here to deliver your gifts, your talents, and your skills
with confidence and inner authority, withholding
nothing. This is when you are living full out, moving in
the reality of love, affluence, and artistry of being. Your
radical aliveness not only affects your individual life but
life on the planet as we know it."

But again, self-doubt was only part of it.
Remember Colin and the external voice? This was a
second barrier for me. Family and societal pressures can be
huge. We've already discussed this with the Voice of
Resistance so I won't go into it again. Suffice it to say,
external pressure can be brutal.

The third reason we bail on our dreams is a misguided paradigm. I used to work with students and coach them on their careers. Countless students bailed on paths that would magnify their talents because of the pressure to get a "real job." We talked about this with the Outside/In, Inside/Out models. When we pursue the real jobs, what we are really doing is pursuing the path of least resistance or the clear path. The path to a job I love is often unsure and unchartered. That's because it is unique to me and I've never traveled the path before! Remember, to get an unconventional job, you have to follow an unconventional path. Suffice it to say that we are often misguided by what we believe an industry is, what a "real job" truly is, and what the path will look like for us to do what we love. As Ralph Waldo Emerson said, "Do not go where the path may lead, go instead where there is no path and leave a trail."

Fourth, we sometimes feel fraudulent. By their very nature, talents take little work. They are innate, natural to our being. As such, we sometimes feel fraudulent using them when others around us work so hard to be good at what we do naturally well. I remember in college doing presentations in classes. Afterward, people would congratulate me on a good presentation and ask how long I prepared. "Prepared? What do you mean?" They would scoff and say they prepared, wrote note cards, practiced in front of a mirror, and got feedback, all to give an average presentation. I simply showed up and went with my gut. The result is that I began to feel fraudulent. Was I really any good at this or were people just pumping my ego? In fact, I actually began to doubt what I did best because it didn't take me as much work as it took others. Examples of this abound.

I have colleagues at work who are natural project managers, calendar organizers, logistics planners, and creative geniuses. They take little forethought or effort to do what they do best, when I take an eternity of bumbling to turn out a half-baked product. They may not recognize their talent, and may actually think it's not that big of a deal. "I thought everyone did it this way," they say. And yet, what they do is innate to them and them alone. I love this idea from Andre Agassi's book *Open*, speaking of those he competed against in tennis:

> "People generally know what they want but they are afraid to pursue it because they can't conceptualize it based on what they know to be true. We know what we want, we just won't allow ourselves to embrace what we want because it's not feasible. The opposite of courage in our society isn't fear, it's conformity. Too many of us conform because, like Shakespeare said, 'Our doubts are traitors, And make us lose the good we oft might win By fearing to attempt.' We fear success in areas that come naturally to us because we don't want to be labeled a fraud when we aren't the best or don't know everything about a subject."

How have any of these four derailers manifested in your journey?

So Now What?

When we first moved to Houston, I would spend about 2 hours in the car between dropping my daughter off at school and commuting back and forth between work and home. That's a lot of time for a tall man to sit in a Honda Civic. Fortunately, I found the ultimate way to pass the time – books on CD. More specifically, I am a sucker for a good Clive Cussler fiction novel. This is probably in part because I am envious of the main characters who are generally oceanographers who traverse Caribbean waters for a living. Sometimes I think I missed my calling in life.

In one of his books, the main character and his squad of do-gooders are preparing to mount an attack against the enemy on a deserted, volcanic island. Just prior to stepping off his ship and into a heated and deadly battle he stops and looks at his reflection in the mirror. The narrator then cites the one truth that has remained consistent about every battle the main character has fought:

> "Facing an enemy means facing yourself. Conquering an enemy gives affirmation to what you always knew about who you are."

Profound. Particularly for a Cussler novel. In the moments of greatest adversity we are forced to face up to who we really are. Our pride and self-assurance often get stripped away, leaving our core self exposed. We dig deep. And by overcoming adversity, our souls are vindicated and validated and we learn about our true character.

Now take the word enemy from the quote and replace

it with "fear" or "adversity" or "mediocrity" and the meaning remains the same. By facing the things that challenge who we are and that get in the way of our success we face our true selves and, if we emerge triumphant, our true selves are affirmed.

So if we know that the result of these battles is that we become more congruent and more whole, then what's stopping us from achieving what we want? Complacency? Comfort? Fear? Insecurity? Take a moment and answer the following:

Q: When was the last time I really faced myself and was forced to tap into the depths of my soul to overcome some sort of trial or adversity?

If you don't have an answer, maybe it's time to introduce some challenge into your life. Dee Hock, the founder of Visa and a writer whose ideas I have followed for some time, once suggested that the most successful organizations are those that have elements of both chaos and order. He dubbed these "chaordic" organizations. I think the same is true for individuals.

Those who seem to grow and progress the most, and achieve a great deal of success, are those who proactively and consistently introduce elements of both chaos and order into their lives.

Now, the majority of us, myself included, probably already have an overabundance of order in our lives – or status quo. What we likely need is an injection of chaos in the form of trying something new: pursuing a new talent or hobby, volunteering for an assignment at work that is outside of our comfort zone, meeting a new person or group of people, visiting an unfamiliar place, or some other form of catalyst. So try something today. Shake up the routine. Stretch yourself. And, in the process, fight our common enemy – mediocrity – and learn to face up to who you really are.

Stop for a moment and reflect on these questions:

> When was the last time you introduced discomfort into your life intentionally? What was it? What was the result?

M. Scott Peck, author of *The Road Less Traveled*, said it well:

> "The truth is that our finest moments are most likely to occur when we are feeling deeply uncomfortable, unhappy, or unfulfilled. For it is only in such moments, propelled by our discomfort, that we are likely to step out of our ruts and start searching for different ways or truer answers."

Start facing your "enemies" today.

The Ugliest Enemy of All

Enemies come in many forms. Let me warn you about one final enemy who deceived me for 25 years. I mentioned it earlier in this chapter but want to expound on it here.

In 2008, I was preparing to graduate with my Master's

degree and was considering several options. I was torn by the decision I had to make and concerned that I might choose the wrong path. I could either A) graduate and enter the workforce, taking my place alongside my fellow working minions who were toiling away for The Man, B) continue on in school for my Ph.D. or "certificate of smartness," or C) travel with the circus as a side show.

As I was considering these options, I met with one of my mentors, a man who was adept at listening and reflecting back to me what I was saying in order to help me work through dilemmas. If you know anyone like this, put them in your pocket and take them wherever you go – they are lifesavers.

I presented my options and told him I didn't know what I should do. That's when he stopped me:

Mentor: "Should" according to whom?

Me: What?

Mentor: You said that you didn't know what you "should" do. "Should" do according to whom?

Me: Hm. Good question. "Should" according to...I don't know.

{Mind blown.}

Mentor: Exactly. We often ask what we "should" do, but "should" implies that there is some societal norm that we are trying to live up to, some standard that we must keep aligned with in order to be acceptable.

You see, "should" suggests a right and wrong. We may ask ourselves what we "should" do, but what we are really asking is "what do I need to do in order to fit the pre-established expectation of 'normal.'"

The Two Ways "Should" Overshadows Our Joy

This "s" word robs us of joy in several ways:

First, we find ourselves constantly fighting to keep up with this invisible expectation while life passes us by.

Second, we become paralyzed by decision-making, afraid of the negative consequences of a "wrong" choice. I have personally experienced the dark days associated with wallowing in what seems like an impossible decision, never feeling like I was going to choose the right path. I was constantly afraid that the path I chose, Ph.D. or workforce, would end up being the "wrong" choice and that I would live with the consequences of my poor decision-making for years.

I could picture myself choosing the Ph.D. and then looking back and saying, "Dang! I knew I should have gone into the workforce." I could also picture myself slaving away under the watchful eye of the "The Man" and wishing I had stayed in school. During these moments, we look at the glass half empty and examine the decisions before us with a "what if" mentality, wondering "what if I choose wrong and hate what I'm doing" or "what if I regret my decision." The clouds move in and rob us of joy. But the way out is simple.

The Way Out

I've heard "should" couched in statements like these:

> "I don't know what I should do when I graduate so I'm going to _____ school." (insert law, medicine, etc.)

or

> "I don't know what I should do for a career."

In both of these instances, and with any "should" question that pops up in your decision-making processes, you "should" do what you think you "should" do. In other words, no one knows you better than YOU. So do what your gut tells you.

There is no ideal roadmap to follow that will get you from point A to point B. In fact, there are many paths that will lead to the same destination. Some may yield more joy than others, and these are probably the paths that allow you to be authentic and do what you do best, but there is rarely a "right" way. Even in leadership the best kind of leader is the person who is authentic, who tries to do what they think is right, and who knows who they are and lives congruent with that knowledge. The moment you try to be the type of leader you think you "should" be you risk inauthenticity.

As my mentor and I discussed this, it occurred to me that there was no predefined path that I "should" follow. It was up to me to carve the path and I chose to do this by following my gut. I strapped on my working boots and headed into the field of leadership development as a practitioner. I never looked back and am happy with where I've ended up. The truth is, I probably would have been just as happy had I chosen the alternate route.

The simple way out, then, is to strip away the "shoulds," make a pros and cons list, and go with your intuition. What I'm talking about is a mindset shift, guiding your mind away from looking at a situation as if there is one right answer and one wrong answer and toward a mentality of accepting the possibility of dueling "goods." The best part about this method is that very few things in this life are final. If one option doesn't work, explore the other. And if that doesn't work, keep exploring.

But I would also venture to say that either option could work because you get out of the option what you put into it. In other words, you construct the option. If I chose the Ph.D., it would have been great because I would have made it great. If I chose the workforce, it also would have resulted in a great outcome. **You are the author of your life.**

So here's what you should do, pun intended. Examine the decisions you are making in your life or look at your life-path in general and ask yourself, "What norm am I trying to live up to? What expectation am I trying to meet?" The answer may be that you are living each day to the fullest and doing what you feel is right for now, and that is great. The answer may also be that you are doing what you think you "should" be doing. In that case, ask yourself "should according to whom?" Then clarify what you would really like to be doing, create a plan, and go for it.

Enough Success to Go Around

Risk is inherent in the journey to utilize your innate abilities and talents. In fact, without risk your talents are known only to you and they may never realize their true potential. As humans, we are not wired to take rejection well and, therefore, it seems that most people have an aversion to risk because of fear of rejection or failure.

There is a remedy: If you know you are doing what you should be doing (according to you, not according to societal norms), you will eventually find success. I've been reading an online book called *Accidental Branding* by David Vinjamuri. The concept is that many entrepreneurs aren't surrounded by the ideal environmental factors to succeed but they find a way to. I would argue that this is in part because they have found congruence between what they are doing and what they were meant to be doing.

Again, from *The War of Art*: "Therefore the more fear we feel about a specific enterprise, the more certain we can be that the enterprise is important to us and to the growth of our soul. That's why we feel so much Resistance. If it meant nothing to us, there'd be no Resistance."

Several years ago, I stumbled upon an article in *Real Simple* by blogger Kyran Pittman entitled "Wear the Corsage" that contained words of wisdom she would have shared with her daughter if she had one. (Don't let the fact that I was reading *Real Simple* distract from the point.) While perusing this little gem, I came across maxim number 16 which also happens to be a principle of leadership that I am passionate about:

> "Live as if there's enough talent, success, luck, and
> fabulousness to go around."

Therein lies a core principle of self-development: there
is enough success and talent to go around.

What you discover about who you are may leave you
feeling vulnerable. You may feel a certain degree of risk
associated with living up to your potential and letting
yourself be who you were meant to be. And yet, it's okay to
fail because there's enough success to go around.

I have a colleague who recently became aware that she
has a real knack for counseling. She is an excellent listener
and provides great insight and feedback. However, by
positioning herself as the token "counselor" she puts herself
in a position to fail to live up to expectations. Now, of
course, this won't happen because she is naturally, innately
talented in this thing. But the risk is present.

The secret to relieving this pressure lies in the maxim
from the article. Living as if there's enough talent to go
around means reminding yourself that everyone is
vulnerable. Everyone has a unique gift or talent that may
require some risk-taking – a leap of faith. Living as if there's
enough success means not fearing failure because there is no
shortage of success for everyone to partake in. Why not
you?!

14 DO IT.

A peculiar thing seems to occur when you embrace your vocation and re-center your life around it. It's as if the universe shifts to allow for more opportunity to put your talents to work. In actuality, the opportunities probably existed all along, but you are better able to identify them because of your heightened sense of self.

Your lens is clearer and the opportunities are all around you to do what you do best. The only thing that stands in your way now is to commit. This isn't an easy journey. It's also not one that many people take, so you won't find many people to relate or empathize. W.H. Murray, a hiker on the Scottish Himalayan Expedition (whatever that is), said this:

> "Until one is committed, there is hesitancy, the chance to draw back – Concerning all acts of initiative (and creation), there is one elementary truth that ignorance of which kills countless ideas and splendid plans: that the moment one definitely commits oneself, then

Providence moves too. All sorts of things occur to help one that would never otherwise have occurred. A whole stream of events issues from the decision, raising in one's favor all manner of unforeseen incidents and meetings and material assistance, which no man could have dreamed would have come his way. Whatever you can do, or dream you can do, begin it. Boldness has genius, power, and magic in it. Begin it now."

Loving your work starts from the inside out. It starts with defining success, becoming self-aware, and consistently doing the Outer Work required to put yourself in a place to be lucky.

"Fortune favors the bold," so be bold. Do it now.

Your Completed Profile

My Inner Voice tells me I was meant to:

Inner Work

My top five values are:
1.
2.
3.
4.
5.

My talents include:
1.
2.
3.
4.
5.

An environment in which I can thrive includes:
1.
2.
3.
4.
5.

Outer Work

Some areas that I want to explore are:

My current constellation looks like (add to it as you go):

Some experiences I plan to pursue are:

Success

My personally defined idea of success is:

I can add value and benefit to others by:

My relationship to money is:

Gauging Risk

In order to pursue my dream, I may have to take some calculated risks. These include:

I will prepare for these risks by:

Is it worth it? Why?

Do It

My next action(s) will be:

I will check in with this supporter regularly:

If I need help, I can turn to:

ABOUT THE AUTHOR

Dustin currently lives in Houston, Texas with his wife and four children. After serving a two-year mission for the The Church of Jesus Christ of Latter-day Saints in Puerto Rico, he set the tone for a happy marriage by failing Dating and Marriage Prep at BYU-Idaho. He then showed why this happened, dragging his family around the nation with nine moves in seven years, all in the name of figuring out what to do with his life. He found his way into leadership development and now works at YES Prep Public Schools training teachers to be leaders and as a private consultant for businesses and non-profits. He especially enjoys helping people figure out their best-fit career and get into it, and spits serious game on the topic at www.dustinpeterson.me. He loves bacon, Dallas sports teams, and long walks on the beach. Email him at dustin@dustinpeterson.me or follow him on Twitter @dustin_lead.